Walking on Eggshells

Confessions from an Asperger Marriage and How We Made It Work

Karen Rowlands

ARC Publishing

ISBN 978-0-9935613-4-4 (Paperback)

ISBN 978-0-9935613-5-1 (Kindle e-Book)

Published by ARC Publishing (Karen Rowlands)

Old Tavern House,
Riding Mill,
Northumberland,
England
NE44 6DX

DEDICATION

To all Asperger wives and husbands out there,
whether they know they are or not

ACKNOWLEDGEMENTS

Thank you to my wonderful husband David who not only let me publish this personal story but also helped typeset it.

I could also not have done this without my proof readers, Val, Tanya, Elizabeth, Trevor and Carole whose different perspective kept my content and grammar right.

Importantly, I would like to thank the members of Hexham NAS who have listened, supported and guided me over the years.

Lastly, I would like to thank my mentors Dr Dawn Benson and David Littlefair from Northumbria University who encouraged me to right this down.

PREFACE

I'm a duck. Paddling frantically beneath the surface whilst appearing serene above the water.

Every day I cope with my own invisible disability whilst also dealing with my husband's and my children. No time to complain.

This book is my outlet.

Who am I?

I am an Asperger wife and mother. This autobiography tells you about who I really am (or was) and how I came to be where I am today.

This is a difficult and challenging existence. When people ask me why I stay, I remind them it is also very rewarding and I would not receive so much love and loyalty from anyone else.

CONTENTS

Rebound

This was a pivotal year. In fact, scrap that; June 1995 was a pivotal month. I finished my degree, finished with my boyfriend of six years and started paying off my student debt. I signed up with a temping agency in Newcastle, who set me up with a typing job with Northern Electric. I managed to get sacked on my first day after admitting I didn't want to be there for the rest of my life. It turned out, what I had assumed was another dreary temporary position was apparently permanent. They had forgotten to mention it to me.

The next assignment was almost as dubious as they asked me if I was any good with numbers. Well, I may have accidentally given the impression that I was after sneaking a fake Maths GCSE on to my CV. I nearly turned the job down but I was feeling the weight of my student debt. After a momentary pause, I accepted and ended up working for an engineering company in an old industrial shipyard on Tyneside.

Thankfully, it turned out my numeric skills were not needed after all but my typing and origami skills were. The work involved sorting documentation for ambitious young engineers. They were industriously designing and manufacturing little ROV's (remotely operated vehicles) for cable-laying ships. My job was to input data, file large drawings and capture the enormous A0 size drawings the engineers were constantly printing off. I would either deliver them to the respective young man or file them in numerical order. I could cope with that.

I was very quickly left to my own devices, in a large room full of printers and one engineer who had not noticed my existence. In contrast, one tall, dark-haired engineer kept coming in carrying hefty computer equipment and setting it up. He noticed me and introduced himself as David. He immediately recognised that I was unsure about what to do next and offered to help me with anything that I needed. He made a good first impression.

The agency told me that lunch would be provided but had forgotten to mention the whole company had breakfast at ten o'clock. Everyone had disappeared for breakfast but David came to collect me. He had noticed I was missing.

I quickly fell in with the company's routine. Everyone worked hard and was very friendly. There was a lot of laughter around the communal dining tables. It was a male-dominated environment, the only other women being in the admin. and accounts departments. I was very comfortable with that as I generally found it harder to be 'one of the girls'. I did get to know Michelle from Accounts quite well as she was near my age. As it was a lovely summer, we would take our coffee breaks outside next to the River Tyne. It was quite idyllic. I would chat to Michelle and the other engineers would bring their mugs of coffee out to enjoy the sunshine too.

On the outside, I put on a cheerful façade, but on the inside, I was desperately unhappy. My boyfriend had messed me around terribly to the point where I had had to finish with him to salvage any dignity I had left. We were at the screaming down the 'phone stage. If the job hadn't provided food on a regular basis I wouldn't have eaten. As it was, I lost a stone in less than a month.

In the evenings, I would be dragged out by a group of friends but I was miserable company. They knew all about my fall out with Tony.

My ex had been living with me and my parents for the last six years until he went to university. He was part of the furniture and my mum was extremely fond of him.

One evening I went out with a couple of close friends and Zach. I had met Zach at college but now he managed a local pub where we were regulars. They managed to get me rather drunk and somehow during the night I ended up holding Zach's hand. He was like the cat who had got the cream. He walked me home and in the dark street of tall Victorian houses, we kissed. I can't say the sparks flew for me but they must have done for him. It all felt very odd for me as though I knew I was single, I didn't feel single. Tony had been living away at university in Sunderland and one of the reasons I had dumped him was because he had disappeared without contacting me for weeks. The only way I could let him know he was dumped was by leaving my engagement ring in his bedroom with a note rolled up in it demanding, "When are you collecting your stuff?". There was no closure.

To top it off, Zach then whispered in my ear, "I can't believe I'm kissing Tony's girlfriend". I've realised since, I'm not the kind of girl that reacts overtly to things that upset me but poor Zach had his card marked. What did he mean? I wasn't Tony's girlfriend anymore; I was me. Had he been coveting me all this time and now Tony was out of the picture, I was the prize? I was fond of Zach but a relationship was never on the cards.

Meanwhile, Michelle had noted that David seemed to be spending an unusual amount of time having coffee outside. This had never been witnessed before. Apparently, he was rarely away from his desk, or indeed, in the sunshine. Aware of my newly single status, Michelle, being a forward kind of Geordie lass, had questioned David and suggested he ask me out.

On a pretext, she got my home number and gave it to him with strict instructions. During the middle of a busy day, she whisked me into the Ladies and asked me if I 'liked Dave. I was rather put on the spot and I'd only been there a couple of weeks. There were a lot of men in the building. I thought I knew who he was, but I had to make sure.

"Umm, which one is he?" I asked. Michelle looked a little disappointed that I hadn't been lusting after him. Well, I wasn't exactly in the mood to lust after anyone. Once she described him I knew exactly who he was. He was the tall, quiet, guy who'd been immediately helpful.

"Is he rich?" I joked. I saw the look on Michelle's face. That did not go down well!

"I'm kidding!" I assured her. I'm very good at saying stupid things when I'm thrust into awkward situations. Wooing eligible engineers was not part of my life plan. Anyway, why would these busy, intelligent men be interested in a poor little student like me?

Not having any reason to hang around in the north east, I decided to leave the job after a month and seek my fortune on the streets of London. I could stay with my grandmother who lived in South London. David, knowing that I was leaving, found the courage to 'phone me and ask me out. I later found out that he would not consider dating me whilst

4

we worked together as he didn't consider that good office etiquette.

I'm not sure why I agreed to meet him for a drink. I think I was flattered but didn't take it seriously. I just thought, "Why not?" He seemed nice enough. Or maybe I just wanted to annoy Tony. David had a lovely speaking voice and came across as confident on the 'phone. We arranged to meet the following day at the Chain Locker in North Shields, a pub near the ferry landing.

Just before I left for my date with David the 'phone rang. It was Tony. It had been weeks since we'd spoken and several days since I'd finished with him. He wouldn't tell me where he'd been, though he was obviously back at his flat. He'd found the ring and my message. We had a blazing row and out of spite I told him I was going on a date and worse, I screamed down the 'phone, "And he's richer than you are!" before childishly slamming the 'phone down.

As I walked down the hill towards the quayside, I saw David drive past me. He didn't wave. I thought that a little odd, but dismissed it. Maybe he hadn't seen me.

By the time he had parked his car, I had caught him up. As he got out, he re-tucked his shirt into his work trousers, I noticed they were about two inches too short for him. I found this endearing but not very sexy.

We sat outside on a bench watching the Shields Ferry coming in and chatted over a couple of drinks. The conversation was mostly about me. I would try and reciprocate with questions but he always turned the subject back to I was infested in. It was like he had a mental questionnaire he needed to get through. The first question he asked was, did I smoke. "No." I was offended at all as I couldn't bear smokers either.

The next thing he asked was my age. I had just turned twenty-four. My birthday had been the catalyst for me finishing with Tony who had barely paid me any attention at all that night. My mum had had to insist he take me out and she even paid for it!

I told David I had gone to university late, at the age of twenty-one. He was quite relieved to find out he wasn't, in his words, 'cradle snatching', as he was the ripe old age of twenty-six. His old-fashioned attitude amused me. I was not used to this kind of thoughtfulness at all. It was a strange mixture of naivety and gentlemanliness.

Unwittingly, I had answered his last question. Well-educated. Tick!

He seemed rather disappointed that I was still determined to move down to London. He gave me his 'phone number and after I had finished my second pint, David dropped me off home, in Alma Place.

When I got in, my dad, not used to passing messages on for his daughter, informed me that Zach had been on the 'phone.

"Oh, what did he want?" I asked, remembering with a wince the other evening.

"He wanted to know where you were. He seemed to think he was your boyfriend," my dad told me rather bemused.

"Oh."

That was rather unexpected and unwanted.

"Did you tell him where I was?" I questioned worriedly. I was cross that Zach was checking up on me. He was making me feel guilty for going out with David. Not that anything had happened. I had not made any promises to Zach and didn't like this feeling of being stalked.

"No, I just said you were out."

I'm not sure if my dad was secretly proud of his suddenly popular daughter or cross with me. He never said. We were both very aware that it was only the week before he had picked me up from Tony's flat in Sunderland. I had been in floods of tears as I left his place for the last time.

The next morning, I was about to get in to the back of my dad's bright orange VW camper van, when Zach appeared. I hadn't rung him back as I didn't know what to say and now, there he was. He seemed to think we were going out. I told him my parents and I were going shopping to the supermarket in Whitley Bay. He didn't take the hint and asked if he could come with us.

I was going to have to tell him. I think I broke his heart. It occurred to me much later, that Zach had been keen on me for quite some time but I hadn't been aware of it. One time that Tony and I had previously broken up, Zach and I had arranged to go to the cinema. Tony found out about it and suddenly we were back together. Years later, Tony admitted he knew about Zach's feelings towards me.

I didn't mention David to him as I wasn't sure what was going on there either. I just said that I wasn't ready for a relationship just yet. It was true.

He asked if he could come in the van with us anyway, as he wanted me to meet his mum. It was all very bizarre but I thought I owed him at least that. She happened to work at

7

the supermarket we were going to and I had a very strange introduction with my not-to-be-boyfriend's mum. I felt a complete cow as he had obviously told her all about me. She was lovely.

In hindsight, I have realised that I am an Aspie magnet. I'm quite certain that poor Zach was not diagnosed with any condition, but one of the first stories I heard about him at college was how he had a meltdown and walked out of an exam. I recognised something in him when we first met. At the time, I probably felt it was our joint goth style and taste in music, but now I realise it was my 'Aspie-dar' was switching on.

Not surprisingly, I didn't see much of Zach after that and I later heard he moved back to Canada to live with his dad.

Before I left the north-east, Michelle persuaded me to come on a works night out, 'Doon the Toon'. We started off at the lively Newcastle Quayside at a popular pub under the Tyne Bridge. David was velcroed to my side the whole evening, ensuring I always had a drink. I don't think I spent a penny all night. Sometimes he was quiet but he had a good excuse prepared. He told me that he was deaf in one ear, due to working backstage as a sound and lighting technician at Birmingham University. I don't know if this was designed to impress me or not but it did add a certain coolness that he was lacking. I was very much into bands such as The Levellers whom he had produced and had some interesting back stage gossip to tell me.

I now know it not to be true. There is nothing wrong with his hearing. However, he does find it extremely hard to follow the thread of a conversation in loud, multi-layered atmospheres such as a pub. It is a form of deafness.

At the end of the evening a few us ended up at another engineer's house in Jesmond. There was only neat gin and vodka to drink. It was quite disgusting, but we were past caring. David on the other hand, was concerned about how I was to get home. I hadn't given it a thought. He decided the best thing was for me to stay the night at his house but first he insisted that I ring my parents to tell them.

Well, not surprisingly, they didn't answer the 'phone. My parents were never the type to sit up all night waiting for me to come in. I only rang them as David insisted it was the right thing to do. David ordered a taxi and took me back to his little house in Gateshead. I was rather surprised when he made up the bed settee in the spare room for me and said,

"Goodnight".

We both had a good night's sleep in our separate rooms and I woke up early with a raging hangover. David drove me home and I crept into the house wondering if my parents had noticed their daughter was a 'dirty stop-out'. As I kicked off my shoes our little terrier, greeted me, but no one else did.

I had no one to mention that night to so I just put it to one side and went off to London, seeking my fame and fortune.

The Streets aren't Paved with Gold

I imposed myself on my Grandma Waterhouse in Mottingham and signed up with some central London temping agencies, waiting for the work to roll in. While I waited, I joined a gym in Eltham and went almost every day. I had a couple of calls from the agencies but they were always last minute and it was impossible for me to get all the way across town in time. I was disappointed and frustrated. At the end of the first week, David rang me for a chat. I told him I was bored and he asked if he paid for my train fare if I would come up and visit him for the weekend.

Well, why not? I thought. Grandma, who was in her eighties, was hardly stimulating company and she kept serving me parsnips with practically every meal. I jumped on the next train leaving Kings Cross and headed north. David picked me up from Newcastle Central station. I hadn't bothered to tell my family I was home for the weekend. They never rang me at my grandma's so I was sure they wouldn't find out. This felt like my little secret. I didn't want them to know what I was up to. It was still early days after breaking up with Tony.

I think quite a lot of wine was consumed that weekend. David was very nervous and desperate to make a good impression. He treated me as if I would break at any moment. I had to teach him how to kiss. He wasn't a natural at all. He didn't know how hard to press with his lips and I'm not sure he liked the idea of sharing saliva. He didn't even know how to cuddle. He sat at the opposite end of the sofa from me and just looked at me. When I sat next to him he just sat stiffly. It was like having a date with a reluctant teenager. I managed to make him relax enough to show him how to drape his arm around me. He must have decided he quite liked it as he did it regularly after that.

That first evening we were both quite tiddly when he started to remove my clothes. Suddenly remarked

"Oh, you're fatter than I thought you were!"

It's a good job I found it funny but it put a halt to anything else happening that night. How different my life would have been if I'd really taken offence and walked out.

I returned to London but spent most of my time on the 'phone to David. Despite everything, I couldn't help it. I was intrigued by the contrast between the confident, intelligent engineer and the shy, awkward boy at home.

The next weekend he picked me up from the station again. This time there was less alcohol involved. I wasn't in a rush and David didn't know how to initiate proceedings. I was intrigued by this paradox and subconsciously there was something about him that I recognised, was familiar with.

That night when we went up to bed it was a bit like a Victorian wedding night. I went off to get changed and David disappeared into his bedroom. We both knew what was going to happen. When I made my entrance into the bedroom, David was sitting up in bed with his navy-blue pyjamas on, as if he was staying in hospital and duvet pulled up to his chin. I burst out laughing and ordered,

"Get them off or I'm not getting in there!"

He quickly did as he was told.

Let's just say that when David confessed that he hadn't done this before, I was hardly surprised. I took things slowly with him and if he wasn't already head over heels in love with me he certainly was by the end of the night.

I on the other hand, was treating this as a rather interesting rebound experiment. It's very hard just to switch off your feelings for your ex of six years, even when you know it's for the best.

Putting on A Pedestal

Sitting on the green carpet he'd chosen with his mum, I was acutely aware that he couldn't take his eyes off me. He sat on the matching green sofa, keeping his distance, whilst he kept telling me I was, "Just perfect".

Obviously, I am not perfect. Far from it, but it was nice to be told so. I don't think Tony had ever said that and it had certainly been a while since I'd had a compliment from him.

It was strangely liberating to be treated like a princess, taken out for dinner, having drinks paid for and complimented regularly. With Tony, I had been the one who had worked and provided a lot of the time.

I liked the way David referred to me by name in conversation. He was obviously proud to be with me. It was good for my self-esteem. We had a lot to talk about and we discovered we had certain interests in common such as music and a dry sense of humour. I found myself growing increasingly fond of him. I refused to call him 'Dave', like everyone else did. That was his work name. To me, he was David. I guess I was already making my mark.

I went back to London, but kept returning for the weekend for a few more weeks. The temping work never really took off and suddenly it didn't seem quite so important. I realised I would have to go home and rethink. Of course, David was pleased and though I had ostensibly moved home, I was never there.

We became totally immersed in each other and I never considered seeing anyone else and it never occurred to me to ask him about his friends and family. One Sunday afternoon I walked down the stairs into the living room to find an unfamiliar woman standing there. She was a smartly dressed, middle-aged blonde, staring at me in amazement. It turned out that this was David's mother. I could tell she couldn't decide whether to express shock or delight on her face first.

She introduced herself as Linda and said that she often popped in on a Sunday afternoon to do his ironing. It hadn't occurred to David to warn either of us about the existence of the other.

She chatted away to me nineteen-to-the-dozen, while whipping through David's work shirts. She didn't stay long. Sunday afternoon was traditionally time to spend with her large family of seven siblings and their offspring. David told me this as if they had nothing to do with him. Even then I could tell that Linda was practically bursting with the need to tell someone.

I was a bit perplexed to find that within a month of getting to know David, he handed me a set of house keys. I don't know whether he believed this was normal or whether he was keen for me to move in. I was still in the stage of getting to know him and to be perfectly honest I hadn't exactly forgotten about my ex either. I hadn't seen or spoken to him at all but I still didn't know whether it was over for good. More than anything, Tony was a habit of six years that was hard to break. I wasn't mentally ready for this kind of commitment. However, it seemed rude not to take the keys.

Little Quirks

There were some things about David I needed time to get used to. For example, he would constantly say Sorry,

13

whenever he thought he was getting in my way, such as when we were cooking. In my mind, if you were in a relationship, the last thing you would do would be to apologise for being in close to the other person. You were meant to take advantage of it! It got extremely irritating and I asked him to stop doing it but he could not. He still does it to this day and increasingly so when he is stressed.

David's little house was a two-bed semi on a new-build estate in Gateshead and it had a disproportionately long front garden. It was next to the path that led to the children's' play area. I soon discovered that the local children didn't like him. They would call him names and he would react. He told me they were 'little shits' and would constantly throw their balls into his garden. His back garden was full of six-foot-high thistles. I had never seen such an amazing display before. I was very impressed by his lack of gardening skills which matched mine perfectly. Shortly after we met though he employed some gardeners to completely pave it over.

I was there one day when a ball landed in the now rather bland, back garden and the kids knocked on the door and asked for their ball back. I found him having a shouting match with a couple of seven year olds and was in the process of confiscating their ball and threatening to burst it with a knife. I couldn't believe it. I removed the ball from him and gave it back to the kids. I couldn't blame the kids for being rude to him. I probably would have been too.

David was insistent that the local kids were deliberately losing their balls in his garden just to annoy him. This was a side of him I hadn't seen before. He was acting like a grumpy old man at the age of twenty-six. I empathised so much more with the kids as we had regularly lost our balls in grumpy old people's gardens when we were kids playing in the streets of Cardiff.

It is often the tiny things that make a person seem different. One of the main ones was when the 'phone rang in the house he always answered as if he was at work with an officious 'Dave Rowlands'. If a friend rang for me, that would throw him into a complete spin. He eventually managed to ask them for their name, but as if he was my secretary. 'May I ask who is calling?' He still does it today. However, I noticed after a few months that progress had definitely been made when he didn't hand the 'phone straight to me but actually had a short, civil conversation with certain, well-known, friends.

Despite these tiny misgivings, I moved in with him and things were very comfortable between us. I should confess at this point that David had still not met my parents. As a parent myself now, I find it very hard to believe that they knew I was living with someone they had never met. Yes, I was twenty-four and yes, he sounded responsible but they never insisted on checking him out. After nearly four months I decided that maybe we were serious enough to let them meet. By this time, even David was curious about my parents.

Before this could happen though I went home a day early. I had to tidy the place up. My parents lived in a six-bedroom Victorian townhouse in a leafy part of North Shields, close to Tynemouth. It was a beautiful house, or it could have been if my mother was at all house-proud. Throughout our childhood she had blamed my brothers and me for the terrible mess in the place. I'm not denying that we weren't messy children but we didn't know any better. Our house was so messy when our friends came around they would be the ones to start tidying up!

I felt somewhat justified that even though we had all left home except for our baby sister, the house was still extremely untidy. By this time, I was quite fond of David and didn't really want to put him off by seeing what a slovenly background I was from. He seemed to think I was rather posh for some reason.

I spent the whole day just clearing up newspapers and toys and moving washing from the sofas and finding the carpets. I vacuumed and cleaned and polished. This mammoth task took place while my parents were at work and it gave me plenty of time to think. It dawned on me that one of the attractions of David was his tiny, minimal house. No clutter and so easy to clean we could do the whole house in what seemed like minutes. Plus, we would do it together which was unusual and refreshing.

David arrived shortly after he finished work, as it was just a short drive from Walker to North Shields. My dad and I were out in the street when he arrived and I saw dad assessing David's new car as it arrived and noting the way he parked it which was rather lazily by driving up onto the kerb and down again.

In the large living room, David nervously perched on a chair and verbally present his curriculum vitae to my parents. I think they were rather amused and bemused by this performance. He was not at all what they had expected. When I had brought Tony home he had long curly hair, a Metallica t-shirt, skin tight jeans and cowboy boots (with spurs) on. In comparison, David had his work trousers, white shirt and black pullover and sensible shoes on. This wasn't just his work wear; this was his everyday wear. He only had one pair of shoes which his mum had bought him.

My mother took a shine to David straight away. I'm not so sure about my dad, but he didn't disapprove. I suspect now that my mum probably recognised in David what I had. She was very forgiving of his odd little ways and I never heard her say a bad word about him.

In the meantime, I never gave up on the thought of a career in London. I joined Newcastle City Council's temping agency, which paid well. I was sent to the newly established Gas Servicing Helpline in Byker. Along with two other girls, I was frontline help for council tenants with a heating crisis. David would drop me off at eight in the morning and sometimes pick me up if I stayed late. There were times that I would ring him at work and he would say he would be leaving in five minutes. He would regularly turn up an hour later having left me standing in the dark.

I would usually get the Metro from Byker and then a bus to our little pad in Gateshead. There, I would potter around enjoying the peace. David often wouldn't be back until after ten, but I didn't mind. I knew that his work was his life and I came from a family where my dad also worked ridiculous hours. Who was I to tell him to work less?

When I lived at my parents' house, especially when Tony lived with us, I would sometimes have to lock the bedroom door to keep him out. He would want to know what I was doing in there. I was reading and having my own space which I needed occasionally. Even today, I revel in that moment when David has gone to work and the kids slam the door as they go off to school. It's just me, the dog and an empty house of peace and possibilities. Bliss.

17

We always had something to talk about but if there was nothing to say, we would have comfortable silences. I've never been one to chat aimlessly and I think it would have irritated David if I had. I knew what work he was doing and always listened and asked questions about his latest project. It helped that I had worked there of course.

Yet, there were occasional strange occurrences to which I didn't know how to react. One evening, David arrived back at the house most distressed. He said he had been a victim of road-rage. Someone had taken a dislike to him in his car and chased him through the streets of Gateshead. At one point the man had got out of his car and started kicking David's door. David had locked all the doors and driven off, driving past the local police station in case the guy was still following him. When I had a look, there were footprints on the driver's door. He was in tears when he told me this and he immediately rang the police to report the incident.

It wasn't that I was unsympathetic but I hadn't been there and I could not understand why he was in such a state. Even when the policeman came around David was upset and tearful. I on the other hand kept out of it and felt quite unemotional in comparison. David seemed to think he was an innocent victim but something just didn't ring true with me. Nothing ever came of it. However, I now know what David's driving is like. He is very mood driven. On the whole, he is an extremely good driver but if he is stressed his driving can be abysmal. His judgement goes, he grinds gears, and he stalls the car. He can also get quite aggressive towards other road users who might not be following the Highway Code exactly. He feels the need to teach them a lesson. He believes he is in the right and justified by his actions.

I have been in the car with him during a road-rage incident, approaching the Metro Centre on a busy bank holiday, where technically he was in the right but hadn't shown any consideration to the other road users and had enraged a man in a four-wheel drive behind us. Instead of ignoring him, David made the situation worse by driving in such a way as to deliberately provoke the driver even more. The driver pulled up alongside our vehicle and was screaming abuse at us through the passenger open window and spat across his wife and on to David's closed window. David just sat there and ignored him. It could have turned very nasty but luckily the traffic was so bad, the incensed man didn't have a chance to get out of his car and through pressure of traffic, went off in another direction. I was extremely annoyed with David as we had the children in the car and anything could have happened. I think we fell out over that because he could not see or admit that he had done anything wrong.

There was another occasion I recall, not long after we had first met, that I remember where I seriously wondered what I was doing with him. I was trying to do something on the computer and asked him for help. He got so frustrated that it wasn't going right he hit the computer tower and a piece flew off it. I didn't say anything but I felt it was a complete over-reaction to a very minor problem. To me it felt the rage had come completely out of nowhere. I think he was just so frustrated as he wanted to help me and couldn't.

I wasn't used to such extreme forms of emotion. My previous boyfriend had been tough, streetwise, laid-back and empathetic in comparison.

I also started to discover he didn't like doing things on the spur of the moment. One Sunday lunch time we decided to go to a pub but he insisted he would not go to a carvery.

Well, it turned out that his favourite pub only served a carvery on a Sunday. He got quite cross about it as if it was a personal insult. He stomped angrily back to the car and started driving around from pub to pub in an increasingly poor mood trying to find somewhere to eat. I ended up getting the blame for the whole thing and I don't think we ever did find somewhere satisfactory to eat. That was the first time he had blamed me for something he considered out of his control. He wouldn't compromise and he wouldn't give up looking for somewhere to eat. I was completely bewildered by his actions and his mood. At the time, I considered it a one off and not the sign of things to come.

On the other hand, David made the most of his other manly traits. There is nothing manlier than being an engineer in charge of multi-million pound projects and huge pieces of machinery. He told great stories of his travelling, going offshore, and working on huge ships; amusing plights that had happened to him and his team in foreign lands.

He was also extremely generous. He never let me pay for anything. The first time we went supermarket shopping he told me to just put anything I wanted in the trolley. Well I didn't, but I appreciated the gesture. When I complained in general conversation about my huge credit card bill of £300 (well it seemed huge to me at the time), he offered to pay it off. I was shocked and refused him point blank. I couldn't let him do that for me. Looking back now, I know that to him general conversation is not just general conversation. When I presented him with a problem he wanted to solve it for me. He probably couldn't understand why I had mentioned it to him if I didn't want him to do something about it, then further confused him by refusing any help.

We would go out for meals and he would never let me pay or even 'go Dutch'. He always had a reason for it. In the end, I just accepted it. We were in a long-term relationship and he earned considerably more than me. Yet there were times that he really annoyed me too. If I was buying a newspaper, just as I was about to pay for it he would suddenly appear at my shoulder and reach over and pay for me. I know he wanted to help but it got increasingly irritating and a little suffocating. I wanted to use my own money as well.

Christmas 1995

Though we were living together by this time, I wanted to spend Christmas with my family, mainly because of my little sister. So, I went out with my brothers on Christmas Eve in North Shields and attended Midnight Mass at Christ Church at the end of our street. It isn't Christmas without singing a few carols.

David went home to the wilds of Kielder in Northumberland, to be with his parents, so I didn't expect him to turn up that evening on Christmas Day. It was a lovely surprise that he had fought his way through the snow and ice to get to me. He spent the time watching old films with us and playing board games with my little sister. It was lovely to see him interact with her. The only time I'd see him interact with children was with his neighbour's kids and that hadn't been good at all.

Up until this point, he had pretty much kept me to himself. I had met his parents and his sister but not the extended family. Most of his family seemed to live in the Durham area, so not far away. His mother was keen that I should meet them. It was traditional for the whole of David's mother's family to get together for a large Boxing Day 'bash'. David had warned me far in advance that this would be quite an ordeal. He had so many aunts and uncles I couldn't keep track of conversations, trying to remember who was who. At least if I met them I could put a face to the names.

With trepidation, we arrived at his aunt's house which was full to the brim with shouting, laughing adults and kids of all ages. I was warmly welcomed, hugged, passed around and interviewed time and time again by his many aunts.

I lost David for a bit after chatting to his aunty Jean for some time but I found him on the floor, building a train set with his young cousin Scott. I thought I had badly misjudged him. Now I realise of course, he was more into building the train set and avoiding adult conversation than actually wanting to interact with the seven-year-old.

Not long after, we had our first real falling out. My parents had been away and we were looking after Sam the dog. I had to go to work so David was entrusted with delivering Sam back to the house in North Shields. I was cooking dinner and discussing arrangements with him at the same time. In hindsight, this was not a good idea. I happened to comment that I would give him my keys when out of the blue he completely exploded in anger at me.

He started ranting and raving at me and I couldn't make head not tail of what he was saying but he was getting more and more hysterical. I didn't know what was going on but at that moment I decided I'd had enough of his unpredictable behaviour. This had come completely out of the blue and I'd had enough. I grabbed my coat and left the house to get away from him.

22

It was a cold, wet and windy night as I marched down the dark street. I was furious and confused at the same time. Why was he behaving like that? I heard him calling my name desperately and he came running down the street in his socks, with tears in his eyes telling me not to leave.

We stood in the street getting soaked as he apologised and begged me to come back. I didn't know if I was leaving him or not but I started to feel sorry for him.

It turned out that when I had mentioned giving him my keys, he had panicked and thought I was returning his housekeys and leaving him. There was absolutely no reason for him to think this. I assume now he probably wasn't listening to me and his first instinct when he picked up on the word 'keys' was a negative one. He was probably living in quiet fear, expecting me to leave him one day. His low self-esteem and simmering paranoia nearly made that happen.

Romance: Aspie Style

The first real test of our relationship came within six months. The engineering project he had been working on was a cable laying ship for a Japanese client. He was expected to go to Japan for an unspecified length of time but he knew it would be a minimum of several weeks. I wasn't sure what this would mean for us but he seemed to expect me to stay in his house while he wasn't there. Then while he was chatting to me about what he would be doing when he was away and how being offshore could be dangerous, he came out with something that nearly ended our relationship there and then.

He turned to me and announced matter-of-factly,

"If I fall off the back of a ship and die, the life insurance will go to my sister and not to you."

I was quietly furious and taken aback. For years after, I didn't know why he said what he did. It may have been an apology that I wouldn't be able to leave me anything if he died. The way I took it at the time I felt he was implying I was a morbid gold digger. Being me my only outward reaction at the time was to say,

"Oh, I don't think I really needed to know that."

Recently, during an interview with a newspaper reporter, I related this story to her while David was there. He had never heard me talk about it before. He looked a bit bemused at my belated reaction to what he had said to me twenty years earlier. I told the reporter how he had made me feel like a gold digger and she turned to David and asked for his side of the story. He replied that in his head, it was his way of saying he wanted to marry me!

In all this time of getting to know him, I would never have come to that conclusion. It amuses me now, as occasionally I'd get a little sad that I never had a proper marriage proposal. Yet it turns out I did. I just missed it!

After David left for Japan, my only form of contact with him was to ring the office to get word to him, which was obviously only for emergencies. In the end, he was away for over six weeks and I lived in the house by myself. I think I had a university friend come to stay for a weekend to keep me company. I did enjoy the peace and quiet of my own company and being in charge of my own home for the first time ever.

The last paragraph probably explains why I am the ideal woman for David. He did contact me whilst he was away. I think once he sent me a fax. Once I got home to find a message on the answer machine and I got a 'phone call from him one evening. He had gone to a lot of trouble just to speak to me. He had borrowed the captain's satellite 'phone and was standing at the topmost part of the ship to get reception on a rolling sea. All I knew was that it was hard work, the food was terrible and he didn't know when he'd be coming back. I suspect he was glad to know I was still there though.

One evening I was cooking a stir-fry when the front door opened with a bang. A man I didn't recognise walked in carrying a large bag. It was David. He had lost so much weight and his hair had grown long, it took me a moment to register who he was.

David told me later that the moment he could escape the job in Japan he literally packed his bag and walked miles to the nearest train station. He crammed himself into a train to the airport and took the first flight home. He hadn't had a chance to ring me. He had half expected me not to be there. Even he realised that his lack of communication was not conducive to a successful relationship.

It was when he walked in that I realised I had really missed him. At that point, I don't know whether I admitted to myself that I loved him but he took two weeks off work and we spent some quality time together. Immediately on returning to work, he then went on a similar trip to Sicily. There he seemed to spend all his time eating pasta and drinking good Chianti and put all his weight back on again.

Chasing the Dream Job

In the meantime, I was buying the Guardian Media every Monday and looking for jobs that would appeal. I applied and had several interviews; the most memorable one being for Dogs Today magazine. I had to write an article and suggest some more ideas before I even got an interview. The money was appalling at £8000 a year and they expected me to survive on that sum in Surrey. I didn't care. It seemed like a dream job; dogs and writing. I thought at the time that I would have paid them to do it.

I stayed at my grandmothers' overnight and caught the train to Woking the following morning. Arriving at the offices, I was immediately set a series of tests. I had to come up with some catchy headlines, that wasn't too bad, write a short article, okay, then I was faced with a set of accounts, my nemesis. Nowhere on the list of criteria had it mentioned being good with numbers. I panicked, spent far too long on the task, and kept changing my answers. I knew I'd failed and was devastated.   However, to rub salt into the wounds, the worst was yet to come.

I was introduced to the editor Beverley Cuddy, who asked me a few questions but then she said she was not the real interviewer and she would go and get him. The real interviewer turned out to be an enormous bearded collie which sat on the sofa next to me. Apparently, if he didn't approve of me I stood no chance of getting the job. Now I am fond of dogs but I didn't take to this one. I thought it was ridiculous that even in a dog magazine that the dog had a say in whom they employed but much worse, was the fact because it was a bearded collie, its face needed a good wash! I think it must have just eaten. It was probably the first dog I'd never wanted to cuddle. I didn't get the job.

David was incredibly supportive and never once did he say he didn't want me to go for these interviews. In fact, he would read through my CV and job application and always give me help and advice.

I must have lived with him for about a year before I got my dream job in London. In the meantime, I was very busy working in gas servicing. I would entertain David with the highs and lows of being on the front line. There was always some tale to regale him with after a busy day.

One month in particular, the media were very hot on the dangers of carbon monoxide poisoning due to several unfortunate deaths being reported. People were warned on TV programmes such as Watchdog that if in doubt to ring British Gas straight away. The following day, we were inundated with calls from council tenants and members of the public. We must have taken nearly four hundred calls each that day.

27

One most memorable one was a little old lady who rang up. Her menagerie was cheeping and squawking down the 'phone behind her, to the extent it was very hard to hear her. It was a bizarre observation of mine but most little old ladies seemed to have cheeping caged birds in the background. This particular lady was very concerned. She said her parrot was ill and she suspected it was dying of carbon 'buroxide' poisoning.' Resisting the urge to giggle, I answered we would send out an engineer to check her boiler but it would not be a priority case and that perhaps she should take her animal to the vet and on the way, buy a carbon monoxide monitor.

Nearly every day we had to deal with old Mrs McNicholas, who we thought at first had been recently bereaved. She would tell us her husband had died and she was cold and couldn't cope. We would send an engineer along as a priority but she would never let him in. It eventually dawned on us she was suffering from some form of dementia and ringing us was part of her routine. We referred her to housing but nothing was ever done about the poor old lady.

Even though this job was not my ideal career choice, the days went very fast as each 'phone call was a different challenge and I got on well with the team of girls and gas engineers. It did a lot for my confidence and communication skills.

A favourite callout for the team was the man who rang to ask if an engineer could come out to remove his gas fire as his iguana had escaped and hidden behind it. We all thought this was very funny, especially when he asked if the engineer could bring a banana to tice it out. The engineer duly did this but the second time the tenant rang, he was not put down as a priority call. There were only so many bananas allocated for in the budget.

To this day, this is one of David's favourite stories that he likes to tell people.

I moved on from Gas Servicing to the heady heights of Housing in the Civic Centre. It was a tedious job and I missed the camaraderie of the girls I had been working with. I was just doing data entry and archiving information. I was so bored I started writing a book which I managed to write during my lunch hour and when the office was quiet.

One late spring morning, David dropped me off outside the offices as usual and by the time I settled in with a cup of coffee and started my computer up the 'phone rang. It was David. He said when he'd got into work he had found out he was being sent to Canada the next day. He was to sort a problem with a ship they wanted to use for offshore work. I asked how long he was going for and he replied,

"Three days."

I teased him by saying,

"Lucky you," and then he completely floored me by asking if I wanted to come. He said he would trade in his business class ticket for two economy ones. I squealed that I would have to ask my boss. My boss walked through the door at that moment and when she found out what I was excited about she generously agreed to my impromptu time off. It wasn't like the work I was doing couldn't wait a few more days.

So, the next day I was swept off to Canada. I hadn't been across the Atlantic before and was very excited. We flew down to Heathrow on an internal flight from Newcastle,

29

again something I'd never done before and spent nine long hours flying to Vancouver. It was all terribly exciting. When we got to Vancouver we transferred to a tiny bi-plane for our last leg to British Columbia. It was the most terrifying and exhilarating journey of my young life so far. I kept looking out of the window to make sure the propellers were still going around.

David took me on the ship with him and we were shown around and welcomed by the captain. We stayed in a decent hotel and had mounds of blueberry pancakes for breakfast. We wandered around the town of Victoria, sampling international cuisine and frozen strawberry margaritas. The whole time, David was the perfect host. He was fun, witty and had plenty to say. There was a lot we didn't see but from where our hotel was we could see mountains with snow in the distance. He promised we would come back one day for a proper holiday. I'm still waiting.

Euro '96

Being a Welsh girl, I'm not keen on football and to my relief, I seemed to have picked the only man from the north east who isn't either! The UK were hosting Euro '96 and several matches were being played at St James' Park in Newcastle. It was impossible to avoid the excitement and atmosphere that struck the city. David and his colleagues had some important clients to entertain and he warned me one evening that he would be out late.

They must have been swept up in the atmosphere in the town as David didn't arrive back until the early hours of the morning. I wasn't worried and didn't wait up for him but I was awoken by him trying to get through the front door. It took him several attempts and then once he was in the house, he crashed around in the kitchen getting himself a drink of water. I was mildly amused by this.

I was less amused when he came stumbling into the bedroom and lecherously tried to grab hold of me, stinking of beer and cigarette smoke. I shoved him off crossly. He wasn't coherent but started flinging his clothes onto the floor. He must have suddenly felt quite ill as he forgot about me and went to the open bedroom window. He stood there trying to get some fresh air for a good twenty minutes, moaning and groaning to himself. This was getting very annoying. Just as I was about to suggest he get some sleep in the spare room, he threw up down the outside wall of the house.

He seemed instantly better and I heard him clatter down the stairs and into the kitchen. Again, there was more crashing and banging and I was wondering what on earth he was doing, when he went out into the back yard and started flinging a bucket of water up at the wall of the house, to remove the vomit. He was making quite a racket. Then he came back to bed and instantly fell asleep, snoring loudly. I lay there wondering what our neighbours saw of my boyfriend, dancing naked in the garden, throwing water everywhere. These new build houses were very overlooked.

I couldn't decide whether to be cross or amused. The following morning, I felt sorry for him as he sat on the sofa looking wan and pale. I'd never seen him so drunk before. He said he'd been led astray by his colleagues and clients who hadn't wanted the evening to end. He had left them all in town and got a taxi home.

The 'phone rang and it was one of my university friends. I started telling her about the events of the night before. As I regaled my howling friend with a description of David dancing in the garden naked, I turned to see him staring at me in horror, blood draining from his face. Until that moment, he hadn't remembered.

Not long after a For Sale sign went up next door.

Return to the Capital

Shortly after getting back from Canada, I had a job interview arranged through an agency at a publishing company in London. I went down for the day on the train. I remember it was a beautiful hot summer's day in June and I walked down from Holborn to the Strand. Cassell was located at the end of Waterloo Bridge and the offices were in a large, beautiful building. My interview with Geoffrey, the Production Director, went well. On a high, I walked down the Strand towards Trafalgar Square and on impulse entered the National Art Gallery. I had time only to wander around the modern art and admire Van Gogh's *Sunflowers* which turned out to be truly stunning in real life. In the gift shop, I bought a less well-known print of Monet's Gare St-Lazare which I rolled up and carried home like a prize. When I got home David thoughtfully framed it for me.

I got the job and had only two weeks to hand my notice in and find somewhere to live in London. Again, David was supportive and we drove down, looking for accommodation. I couldn't believe some of the awful places that people lived in. We walked into one house share in Tooting which was filthy, with only a mattress on the floor. I could see the absolute horror on David's face which was probably reflected on my own. We couldn't get out of there quick enough.

Eventually, I found an advert for a room in a house in Streatham. A lovely, heavily pregnant Afro-Caribbean lady called Michaela lived in the house and the room for rent was large, well decorated and overlooked a pretty garden. David signalled his approval and I took the room. He drove me back down to London with all my belongings two weeks later.

I wasn't daunted at all by moving to London. It was what I'd been dying to do for over a year, not for the place itself but to get started on the career ladder I had dreamed of. The salary of a production assistant was truly terrible, though marginally better than a dogsbody in Woking. There were promises of swift promotion and training and I was looking forward to it.

The first few weeks of my new job whizzed by. I had so much to learn and I made friends with Alice who was also a recent graduate. She had been there a few months longer and had found her feet. We got on well as she showed me the ropes. A new Production Manager arrived in our department but she didn't last long. I really liked her but she was out of her depth. She had been working in the printing industry and had been head-hunted to work with Cassell but she confided in me that she didn't fit in. She felt she was too working class and that everyone else was very middle-class and 'Oxbridge' educated. This wasn't entirely true, and I was sorry when she handed in her notice.

I was settling in, despite missing David, getting used to my daily commute and what I considered easy office hours of 9.30 to 5.30 after my long days working for the council. It was a completely different working style in London. No one thought anything of you going out to lunch and coming back a bit tipsy. Suppliers regularly took even lowly office girls out for lunch to decent restaurants. This was handy as it meant I didn't have to cook much when I got home.

Things started to go wrong for me when the new production manager arrived. Sandra was in her fifties. She was tall, slim and elegant and called everyone 'Darling'. She smoked a lot and had a hat called Gerald. We went to the pub on her first evening and Alice, who worked for Geoffrey and I thought she was lovely. We were wrong.

In hindsight, I think she felt threatened by me. She didn't want a young, enthusiastic assistant who might take some of her glory. The only thing she ever asked me to do was menial tasks like photocopying, counting slides or collating. She would leave Post-It notes all over my desk in the morning, demanding two copies of the paper it was stuck to. It would have been faster for her to have copied them herself but I knew she was making a point. What the point was I had no idea.

If I ever made a mistake she was unforgiving and when things did go wrong that had nothing to do with me, I would still get the blame. I was a quiet, shy person and found it hard to stand up to her. She would put me down in front of suppliers and never apologised if it turned out she had accused me wrongly. Inside I was very angry.

I would regularly be on the 'phone to David whingeing about my job and telling him how miserable I was. He never had much to say and I could tell he felt awkward talking about personal problems during work hours. I started to go home every weekend even though I couldn't afford it. David happily paid for my train fare but what he didn't tell me at the time was that he couldn't afford it either.

To make matters worse, my accommodation in Streatham which had started out well, became a nightmare. Michaela's boyfriend and father of her unborn child also lived there. The family were Ghanaian, and at first were friendly and welcoming. Her boyfriend had offered me lifts to places and was very chatty. I mostly kept to myself and didn't interact with them socially, especially as I was never there from Friday morning to Monday night.

One hot summer night I was abruptly woken by my bedroom door banging open. Michaela came running screaming into my bedroom, massively pregnant in just a night shirt. Her boyfriend was chasing her and dragged her out by the hair yelling, "Why did you go in there?" at her.

Under the bed covers, I hadn't been wearing anything as it had been so hot or I told myself I would have immediately have jumped up to help. The truth of it was I was terrified for her but also for myself. He had dragged her back into their bedroom next door and was hitting her. I heard him smash the telephone when she tried to call her family for help. I didn't know whether to creep downstairs and call the police or go in and interfere. In the end, I'm ashamed to say, I didn't do anything even though the shouting went on for a long time. I had nowhere to go and was worried he would turn on me too.

The following morning after very little sleep, Michaela knocked on my door. She had a swollen face and a black eye and apologised for waking me, dismissing the whole episode as a misunderstanding. We didn't look each other in the eye. She didn't ask for help. I was ashamed for not offering help.

At work, I shakily told Alice what had happened the night before and why I was so tired. She invited me back to her place for the night which I eagerly accepted. After that, I started staying out for as long as possible. I would go and see films in Leicester Square by myself or when Alice invited me to stay over at their shared house in Tufnell Park. It was such a relief to spend time with her and her lovely, impish, sister, Lucy.

Occasionally I would go and visit my eldest brother Rhys, who worked as director of a computer company in Richmond. It was nice to see him and occasionally, I'd get invited out with him and his work mates. We would often meet up in the pub nearby. He would never arrive on time. I would have to walk to the 'phone box outside and ring him to remind him I was there. Then, when he did turn up he was always very generous but he would insist on talking to me about his work. I could generally keep up for the first few sentences but my eyes would start to glaze over after a while. He could never talk to me in layman's terms. Once he asked me if I understood and I confessed I hadn't understood anything for the last half hour. He wasn't offended. He just proceeded to describe to me in detail, complex algorithms all over again.

Sometimes, I would mention to Alice that I was going to meet my brother for a drink and ask her if she would like to come. Mainly because I would have someone else to talk to but a small part of me was aware they were both single. She always declined.

One evening, I told Rhys about my terrible housing situation. He said his secretary Heloise lived in a big house in Kew and was looking for a lodger. This was a godsend. I had met Heloise and got on well with her. I moved in to my own room and bathroom in the top floor of their Victorian house.

The day I was due to move out, Michaela said she was going to the bank to return my deposit to me. I had made the mistake of paying her a month's rent in advance as well as a deposit but she said I would get it back. David waited with me for Michelle to come back but after quite some time we realised she wasn't coming back with my money. I just wanted to leave. David was cross for me and talked about taking some of her things until she returned my deposit but I just wanted to get out of there. I've since discovered that David is 'all mouth and no trousers' and likes to say daring things but would rarely carry them out.

Once again, he helped me move and was relieved that I had found a better place to live. Considering his opportunity, he didn't take advantage of it and didn't ever once suggest that I come home.

The commute to work from Kew was must easier and quicker, straight along the Northern Line to Embankment. Heloise had three children, a quiet but rather odd husband and two boisterous terriers. My accommodation had improved but my work life was going from bad to worse. I had an appraisal with Geoffrey who was perfectly aware that I was having problems with Sandra. I was honest with him and though he was sympathetic he told me I would just have to try harder. I said I had learned to be one step ahead of her but she never appreciated it and Geoffrey's only advice was to become three steps ahead of her. This was difficult as no one was prepared to teach me anything anymore or let me have any responsibility. Sandra had blocked the pay rise that I had been promised and one I desperately needed.

Living in Kew started off well but slowly but surely it all started to get a bit weird. I never felt very welcome downstairs. I felt very much in the way if I tried to cook in the kitchen. It was their family home. I avoided any rooms other than my bedroom in the loft and the bathroom I ended up sharing with the Spanish au pair.

At the same time, Heloise would come and talk to me about the problems she was having with her teenage daughter. She didn't know how to control her and stop her going out at night. I listened to her but tried not to give her advice. It wasn't my place.

The husband, Clive, never spoke to me. He seemed to have an office downstairs but I'm not sure he ever did any work. I think Heloise was working full-time to keep the family running. On my way out one day, I came across the kids huddled around Heloise who was collapsed on the hall floor. She looked like she was unconscious. I immediately reacted and asked if she was alright and what had happened. The kids just looked at me and said,

"She does this all the time. She'll be fine."

I looked at them a long moment with their sad, serious faces and the unmoving Heloise. Was she dead? Had she fainted? Or was she faking it to pay the kids a lesson? It didn't feel like they wanted me to interfere so I went on my way. Turned out she wasn't dead but I never found out what was going on.

The glamorous world of publishing wasn't working out quite as I had planned but it wasn't all bad. Sometimes I got to meet or speak on the 'phone to famous and bestselling authors such as Nick Hornby and Terry Pratchett, both of whom I was in awe of. One day we had a visit from LeVar Burton of Star Trek the Next Generation and Alice and I fought over who was going to make him a cup of coffee. I won but unfortunately, I gave him a mug that still had someone's lipstick on it. Oops!

My depressed moods got to the point where I was becoming quite tearful on my weekends at home and once where I would have been getting the train back on a Sunday afternoon, I was now staying the night and David was driving me to Newcastle station to get the first train out to arrive in Kings Cross for 9.00 am. I would arrive in the office with my rucksack, probably looking a bit dishevelled after trying to sleep on the train.

Sandra noticed how despondent I was and that I was going home every weekend. She saw this as a lack of commitment. I think she expected me to stay to ridiculous hours of the night like she did, but there was no point as I had no responsibilities and I hated it. I didn't realise at the time how down I was I started to make more and more mistakes. I couldn't even count the same number of photographic slides twice.

Depression

Looking back now I wasn't in a good way. I would quite often buy a bottle of wine on the way home from work and never much food. I probably convinced myself that I wouldn't drink all of it that night, but often, I did. I had never drunk much as a student; I couldn't afford it but I had got into the habit of drinking in the house with David.

Before Sandra had arrived, my job had been interesting and challenging. Geoffrey had trusted me to do a lot more but after Sandra it all went backwards. She saved money on the printing by not having the proofs collated, so when the packages of book covers arrived, I had to spend hours walking around the boardroom table manually collating the prints. This of course was false economy but it got me out of Sandra's way. I was so tense and miserable and wondering where my life was going whilst doing this, I got a repetitive strain injury. It started in my neck on the right side as a twinge but gradually, over the weeks, it worked its way down my arm and my back. I couldn't sit comfortably for long and I couldn't sleep without having to lie on my front with my arm behind my back. I was in agony.

My brother, Nick recommended that I see his chiropractor one weekend and made an appointment for me. I was a little dubious but was ready to give anything a go. Alan and his manipulations gave me a lot of relief from the pain and tension straight away. He warned me it would hurt a lot the next day and it did. Despite that, I felt like a new woman, at least until I got back to work.

Chain-smoking Sandra was not above making rude remarks about my weight or appearance. One lunch time, I came back from a very expensive hair appointment in a little salon off the Strand. She was giving me instructions on what to do when she stopped mid-sentence and stared at me. My hair had grown and was quite long and I had had a significant amount taken off and styled.

"You've had your hair cut!" she exclaimed.

I waited for the insult.

"It looks surprisingly good."

That was the only compliment I ever got from her.

On the run-up to Christmas the suppliers and printers would generously send us gifts or bribes. The Spanish printers sent us several cases of Rioja and the Italians sent us Panettone and other goodies. Other suppliers would send large boxes or gold-trimmed Belgium chocolates. These were always welcomed by the office staff who would share them out. I had never seen such generous delights before as bribery never happened at the council. Alice and I were having a good inspection of the chocolates when Sandra, who had had enough of this frivolity, demanded loudly,

"Karen, if you could tear yourself off the ceiling for a moment. We have work to do."

It seemed it was fine for everyone else in the office to relax a little at Christmas but not me.

The chocolate sat on the table between Alice's desk and mine. I never took any chocolates, partly because I'm not a big fan but mainly I didn't want to give Sandra the satisfaction of making comments.

She however, would come and stand at the large box for minutes at a time and discuss the finer qualities of each delicacy with Alice who, unlike me, was an avid chocolate fan and then walk away. I never saw her eat anything. Just smoke.

At Christmas, I took a week off and went up to Kielder where David's family lived, officially the most remote village, not just in Northumberland but in England. It snowed heavily at New Year and when I should have gone back to London I rang them and said I was snowed in. It was a complete lie. David would have easily taken me to the station if I had wanted to go.

Karma

We had a shipment of precious prints arrive very late one week and they were due to be collated by me and then quickly presented at an important meeting. I brought the large package up from the post room and Sandra pounced on it. She snatched the Stanley knife out of my hand and ran it through the packaging in a hurry. I gasped in horror as I saw that she had scored straight through the expensive prints which had not been well protected by the brown paper. She was so angry but for once she couldn't be angry with me. That made my day! She could see the joy in my eyes and she knew she couldn't lay the blame at my door as it had been witnessed by the whole office. Karma at last!

One morning before work I stood up too quickly and smacked my head on the low wooden beam in my garret bedroom. It really hurt! Normally I would have cursed a bit and carried on, but this time I started to cry and couldn't stop. I must have cried great gulping sobs for about ten minutes. I think all the angst of the last year suddenly poured out in that moment and banging my head so hard gave me the excuse to cry. I obviously needed the release as

I hadn't talked to anyone about my situation, other than David who was no use at all.

I started thinking about looking for another job but my confidence was so low I couldn't see the point. One weekend in February I had a heart to heart with David which mainly involved me talking at him. I said I was thinking of quitting but didn't know what I would do next. I wanted him to support me more emotionally but he said he didn't know how to help. I thought he just wanted me to quit and come home and not look for another job but he wouldn't say either way.

I can't recall who brought the subject up. It's hardly the most romantic proposal in the world but we decided to get married and this would be the reason for me coming back. David was over the moon. My one ultimatum was that we would have to get a dog. David who had never had a dog or a pet in his life, readily agreed. I think he would have agreed to anything to have me back permanently.

I wrote my letter of resignation to Geoffrey that weekend and returned to London happier than I had been for months. I quietly told Alice my plans. She was hardly surprised, but very sad to see me go.

A month later, Alice and I organised a small leaving party in our office and a lot of people came from surrounding departments. I gave a speech where I thanked Geoffrey profusely for everything he had taught me over the last year or so. The official line was that I was leaving to get married but everyone knew I was leaving because of Sandra. According to Alice, after that a few girls came and quickly went, none of whom could cope with working with Sandra. I wonder now, looking back whether Sandra should have been pitied. She was anorexic, critical, anxious and paranoid, with apparently no friends. She quite possibly was a candidate for a diagnosis of Asperger's Syndrome, but I'll never know.

On top of this, things were not going well at home for my parents. My most prominent memory was Nick 'phoning to tell me that mum had been diagnosed with breast cancer. This was devastating news. However, mum was incredibly brave and had a mastectomy, chemotherapy and radiotherapy whilst continuing to work. I was very proud of her. Looking back, I feel guilty for not having been there as much as I could have for my parents. I was caught up in the traumas of my own life. I was much more selfish in those days.

My dad was also having problems at work. The reason we had moved to Newcastle in the first place was because he was forced to take voluntary redundancy in 1988 from Cardiff University. He had lost his security and job for life. At the time, not surprisingly he had a few meltdowns. We had seen them building up but understood what a terrible stress and change it was for dad, especially as his fourth child had just been born and his eldest child had just started university. He was given a large pay-off but he knew it wouldn't last for ever and he was convinced he was written off as he was in his forties. However, he had an academic paper to give at a conference in Germany. He'd had a whole year to write it but he hadn't motivated to do so. He hadn't wanted to go but my mum insisted that he did. Dad sat outside the conference on a park bench and wrote the paper shortly before he had to deliver it. From that speech, he was offered a job by a professor at Newcastle University.

This was a lifeline for dad, although it must have been distressing for mum who had to move three hundred miles north, away from all her friends and community. The problem with dad's job was that it was not another tenured position but was on a rolling, yearly contract. It was not a teaching position like he had been used to. He had always lectured and dealt with students and he had always had the same room in the building in Senghenydd Road to work out of. Consistency. This role was in a research unit at Newcastle university. It was a new operation, and the Professor's baby. Dad's office was moved from the maths department to engineering and back again, before they settled into the building on Claremont Road.

He had to deal with many more people and apply for work from companies all over the UK. It was not the comfortable, stable atmosphere of maths. geeks he was used to. There was no certainty. From the first six months of his contract he would be enthusiastic and industrious and nice to know, but as the time ticked down to when he would find out if his contract would be renewed he would get stressed and increasingly anxious and I would avoid him. He could not cope with this new and precarious position. I felt I often got the brunt of his anger and anxiety. I suspect in hindsight it was my mother who got all that.

After nearly ten years of him suffering from this cycle of stress I think he burned himself out. Being in a constant state of fight or flight was too much for him. He was diagnosed with depression and was on long-term sick leave.

At the house in North Shields, I sat in the kitchen with mum and told her that David and I were getting married. She didn't leap for joy. This was the second time I'd told her I was getting married. The first time, my boyfriend and I had been seventeen and I had made a naïve romantic gesture and asked him on February 29. I hadn't planned it. I assumed he would take it as it was meant; a joke. Unfortunately, he said "Yes!" and then told his parents. I didn't know how to get out of it. When we stood hand in hand in front of my parents and told them, I was visibly cringing. I knew they would disapprove. Thankfully, they didn't give me anything to fight against so it just naturally petered out. I should give my parents more credit for being wise occasionally.

This time, mum took me seriously. She thought for a moment and then asked me if I loved him. I too paused before I replied with a firm,

"Yes".

Was that her far too subtle way of telling me that I was doing the wrong thing? That she felt he was far too like my own father and she alone knew what that meant? She knew that we were happy and she knew that David adored me, so she didn't have valid grounds to try and dissuade me. Yet her instincts were obviously telling her that her daughter was getting into a similar situation that she had found herself in.

I knew this wasn't the overwhelming, electric, devouring, teenage love that I had had at the start of my romance with Tony. I was older and wiser and knew that I wanted more from a man than puppy-dog eyes. I knew I could trust David and that he would always be there for me and that he loved me unconditionally. For me, it wasn't an instant chemical reaction but a long, slow realisation that this was what I was looking for. I was attracted to his intellect, reliability and quirkiness.

David kept his promise to me that I could have a dog. I looked around for some time determined to get a Welsh

Springer Spaniel like the one my parents had bought me for my eighth birthday. After much searching, I discovered a local breeder just a mile up the road in Whickham. We went to see him and I came away with an eight-week-old wriggly pup that I named Dylan. I nearly put that we named Dylan but David didn't have any part in that decision at all.

It was a lovely summer and Dylan would play out on the lawn. The kids whom David hated, suddenly became our best friends as they wanted to play with our cute little puppy. Suddenly David didn't mind them. Before my existence in his life, he had just considered the children annoying little aliens. Once they started asking questions about the dog he was surprisingly fine with them. He had started to see them as people.

Our front garden wasn't fenced in and it had a long drive right up to the garage by the front door. Though David never used the garage for the car, he did park it at the front door and would reverse right down the drive when leaving. I was washing up in the kitchen when David decided to pop to the shops. Dylan was playing in the garden by himself. I thought to myself that David will check to see where Dylan was before driving away and then I suddenly knew in my heart of hearts that he wouldn't.

I rushed out of the front door to see David reversing and Dylan sitting right behind the moving wheel, staring obliviously down the drive. I screamed,

"Stop!"

and David immediately slammed on the brakes but didn't know why. Thank God, he hadn't questioned me. He got out of the car and said confused,

"What?"

but I had already scooped the unharmed pup off the tarmac. He was literally just behind the tyre. David turned pale and didn't know what to say. I started to shake as I realised what I'd just averted. I'm so glad I listened to my instincts in that moment.

Dylan was very good for me as I didn't have a job it meant I could concentrate on him for a few weeks. He helped me get over the stress and depressive cloud I had been under for a long time. I soon bounced back to my normal self and started looking forward to our wedding and making plans for the future.

I approached several local advertising agencies as the publishing industry turned out to be almost non-existent in the north. Somehow, none of the interviews I set up worked out. I think I knew in my heart that advertising was not where I wanted to be. I didn't have the right personality. I wasn't gung-ho and 'gobby' enough.

I got a secretarial job at Durham University; first in the English department working for the professor there, and then in the Theology department. David would drop me off at Newcastle Central Station in the morning and I would catch an East Coast train to Durham. Surprisingly, I found I enjoyed myself in that department as they let me have creative free reign with many of their documents. They appreciated my flair and slowly, I felt my self-confidence returning.

After work, I had a bit of trek as I would walk back to Durham station, catch the train to Newcastle and transfer onto the Metro. All this to get to my parents in North Shields. David would drop the puppy off with my mum for the day so he wouldn't be alone and then pick me and Dylan up in the evening when he had finished work. It was good to spend time with my parents and little sister in a more grown-up way. My relationship with my parents improved vastly after I moved out.

One day, I got to North Shields after work to pick up Dylan only to find my mum in a state. He had disappeared. There was a gap in the old wooden back gates and he had escaped through it. She had been looking but couldn't find him. She was hoping he would just come back. He was only four months old. I was furious with her and desperately upset about Dylan. I walked the streets and back lanes for ages, terrified the now gangly pup had been run over. I eventually made my way to the police station. I had to stand in a long queue to be seen and I couldn't help it; I had tears pouring down my face. Someone noticed and thought I must have been attacked and offered to let me take their place. I thanked them but refused, sobbing that I had lost my dog. I didn't get much sympathy from the police but they took my details.

By the time I'd walked back to my parents, there had been a 'phone call from the police. One of our neighbours had found him hours before. I ran along the road and they let me in and there he was, sitting happily on their sofa, wrapped in a blanket. He was quite pleased to see me but I think he would have happily stayed there if I hadn't come for him.

Early one Monday morning in September, I was making my way up the steep hill by the riverside. The narrow path led up to Palace Green and Durham cathedral. The weather was terribly grey and foggy and I could barely see more than a few yards ahead of me. As I turned the corner into an ancient alleyway leading from the riverside walk to enter the mediaeval grounds, I stopped in my tracks, terrified. Two women in Tudor dress came drifting towards me. I couldn't see their feet and the morning mist was swirling around them. They had headdresses on and wide mediaeval skirts with layers of petticoats. They were chatting quietly. They nodded to me as they passed. I was frozen to the spot.

My heart nearly gave out until I remembered that the famous director, Richard Attenborough was on location and had booked the university grounds that week. We had been warned there would be disruption while filming took place. They had chosen this historic cathedral to film some atmospheric scenes for the epic, *Elizabeth*. I had forgotten.

I was a little distracted from my work that week as my window overlooked the green and I saw actors such as Cate Blanchett and retired footballer, Eric Cantona, strolling around in fantastic gowns talking on mobile 'phones.

Wedding Preparations

During this period, David and I were in perfect harmony, or so it felt. We discussed everything and didn't disagree on much. I wanted to get married in a church. A Register Office would have no meaning for me. Though David is a devout atheist he says he believes in the rights of people who want to have a faith. He was more than happy to do this for me. He even went to his local church in Gateshead to hear the banns being read. My mum went with him and to his horror it turned out to be a 'happy clappy' church, the worst kind in his eyes. I can't imagine what was going through his head during that service as they got the guitars and drums out! He said my mum enjoyed it though.

We hadn't considered a budget for the wedding and it never occurred to either of us to ask our parents for anything. It was our wedding. So, I was rather touched when my dad surprised me by announcing that we could have a small budget of £4000 towards the wedding. My dad never reached into his pocket without being asked and I had learned never to ask. My mother may have had something to do with it.

When I asked David what type of wedding he envisaged, I don't think he cared at first. We had recently been to a town hall wedding and neither of us was impressed. It was devoid of atmosphere. We decided that most important to us, was that our friends could come, some of whom we hadn't seen for a long time. A guest list of sixty, which included close family and our dearest friends, was settled on. Rhys would have to fly back from New York where he had settled and my best friend Beckie, was delighted to fly back from New

Zealand where she had been living and teaching for a few years.

We searched the traditional venues but they were expensive and not exactly what we were looking for. On Linda's suggestion, we went along to Broomley Grange. It was a big old house in private grounds and this really had seen better days but was magnificent in its own way. The staff were very friendly and helpful and we discovered as it was an old Boys' Brigade centre. We could hire the whole place and accommodate thirty guests to be fed and watered for the whole weekend for half our budget. David, mum and I looked at each other and knew this was exactly what we wanted. It was perfect.

My mum attended Holy Saviours' church in Tynemouth, and occasionally I would attend too. The vicar was a friendly chap called Richard but when he asked us about children we both said we didn't want any. Well that was how we felt at the time. We hadn't considered it at all.

I was a little disappointed the church didn't have a choir, but it didn't matter too much as they had a good organist and I was bringing my own Welsh choir with me in any case.

To save money we created our own cream and gold scrolled wedding invitations and matching order of service. I chose the hymns, some good Welsh ones such as *Love Divine*, the *Blaenwern* version of course. I knew my friends and relatives would do me proud. Because David had few friends and wasn't overly keen on inviting extended family, we decided it would be silly to have 'sides' in the church and our ushers were encouraged to just mix it up a bit. David did however invite two very good university friends of his, Martyn and Sally, who were married and had recently had a baby. The first time I met them was on the eve of our wedding. Sally later confessed to me that she was so relieved that I was 'normal'. She was worried that David would find a girl more like him.

I knew Sally had meant a lot to David at university and she may have been his first crush. He used to be her guardian angel by the sound of it; rescuing her from nightclub toilets when she had drunkenly managed to fall asleep and lock herself in and other similar escapades. I don't think David drank a lot and as he was that rare student with a car, he was often the designated driver.

Sally's relief at meeting me reminded me of the first time I had met David's sister. Jane was a year younger than me and a medical student at Liverpool University. David had once shown me a picture of his sister, a vivacious looking blonde. He was obviously very proud of her achievements, but hardly ever mentioned her. Shortly after we got together, he announced Jane was coming to visit. As usual, I would be home from work first so I was to let her in. When the bell rang, I opened the door with slight trepidation and was greeted by a rush of blonde hair and a bottle of wine. She was a lot of fun and very chatty, the polar-opposite to her serious brother.

My mother was more nervous about the wedding than I was. David and I had organised it and the whole reception. We did not expect anything to go wrong.

Neither of us had much of a stag or hen party. We weren't interested, but my friends did come and stay with us a few days before the wedding and we went out for some lively meals and drinks.

I hadn't communicated with my ex-boyfriend in a long time. There was no need really. Occasionally, Nick and I would privately mention him and worry about how he was getting on. I felt a certain amount of guilt as he had no family to support him. Other than his student digs, Tony had nowhere to live. Selfishly, I felt I needed to see him one last time to make sure in my mind I was doing the right thing. Marrying David was a big step. There would be no going back. I needed to be sure that I wasn't still on the rebound. It seemed only fair I tell him in person. We arranged to meet in a local park. I wasn't sure he would turn up but he did. It was very odd seeing someone I had known and loved for so long. He looked just the same in black jeans and boots with heavy jewellery. He had just graduated.

I felt nothing.

In some ways, it was as if nothing had changed as we talked easily but the chemistry was no longer there. My heart had gone elsewhere. That was a great relief to me. I could get married with a clear conscience.

Wedding

Most of our guests travelled and arrived on the Friday night. The accommodation was available all weekend and the bar was open. David and I went along to catch up with friends and family we hadn't seen for ages. It was fantastic having the run of Broomley Grange to ourselves. Someone found a piano and a hymn book and we had an impromptu choir practice. Everyone was smiling and laughing and I felt lucky and very loved.

That evening before I left, I had a quiet word with my brothers and close male friends to ask them a favour. Alice and Lucy were arriving on the train from London in the morning and they didn't know anyone. I asked them to keep an eye out for the girls.

I had to force myself to leave so I could get a good night's sleep.

The night before the wedding we were traditional and I stayed with my parents in North Shields. I didn't get the best night's sleep as my sister's cat decided to spend most of the night sleeping on my head.

Jane and her boyfriend stayed with David as she was his best (wo)man. David had been in a quandary about who to ask as his best man. He hadn't wanted to offend anyone. I had suggested he think outside the box and ask his sister. In that way, no one would be offended. Jane was delighted to be asked.

October 18th, 1997 dawned a crisp, clear and sunny day. I had no doubt that my bridegroom would turn up. We didn't waste money on fancy cars. We simply had his Renault valeted and my brother Nicholas was chauffeur for the day.

My dress had been created by my wonderful Italian godmother and I had chosen a golden material with cream lace detail. I adored the dress that had been designed and lovingly hand-made by Maria. I would say it was unique.

The main worry that day, was whether dad was going to be relied upon. He still hadn't returned to work, and indeed was considering early retirement. He was only fifty-five. I didn't put any pressure on him at all and a few days before he decided he was well enough to give me away. It would have been a difficult day for him with the extended socialising. In fact, the socialising probably took place across four days, but because we had only invited close family and friends he was actually very comfortable with most people and I think it helped his mental health. Moving away from Cardiff, we had left so many lovely people behind. It was heart-warming for dad to know that people still loved and cared about us.

He looked so smart and happy on the day of the wedding and was very proud to walk me down the aisle. He didn't say too much. He didn't have to.

Standing in front of the altar with David, I had no qualms. I held his hand tightly as he was shaking with nerves. The vicar gave a little talk on having children with an apologetic smile to us. Apparently, our friends had taken bets that we would have our first baby within two years. Damn them; they were right!

In the church grounds after the ceremony people were perhaps surprised we didn't have an official photographer. It was an expense we decided we could do without. We asked everyone to take plenty of photos and we made our own arrangements. It was great fun and very relaxed.

Broomley Grange

We coached our guests back to their accommodation and reception venue at the large country house just outside the rural village of Stocksfield in Northumberland. To the delight of our elderly guests they were all offered cups of tea when they arrived back, which probably also helped the younger guest who had nipped to the pub before the ceremony. People kept insisting on taking photographs of me in my dress and I remember standing on the grand staircase by myself staring down at the huge crowd around me. David didn't care to have his photo taken with me. It's only just occurred to me that we could have had some lovely couple's photos of us taken together in the grounds of the house.

We had organised the caterer from David's work, to provide a Mexican meal as neither of us wanted a traditional set-up. At one point, I felt very overwhelmed and didn't know why. I remember David coming up to me and asking if I was alright. I told him I was but he could tell I was lying. I don't think I like being the centre of attention. I needed a moment to myself.

It was a very relaxed atmosphere with a lot of mingling and we did not make any speeches other than Jane who stood up to give her best man speech. I rather belatedly learned some interesting things about my new husband's childhood.

She regaled her avid audience with the story of David's imaginary friend, Douglas. When David was three, before Jane was born, he and his mum had been travelling on the bus and when they got to their destination they got off. Just as the bus was moving off David got upset and told his mum that Douglas was still on the bus. Linda knew instinctively that he would not be calmed unless she took him seriously. To David, Douglas was real. What a great mum she was. Linda had to stop the bus and run right to the back seat and pretend to grab Douglas as the only way to placate her child. This story went down extremely well to a room of slightly inebriated guests. Little did I and the audience know that this is one of the early signs of an autistic child.

My elder brother Rhys, took me at my word and made sure that Alice was duly looked after and entertained. After the meal, he took a couple of helium-filled balloons from the table decorations and walked across to her. He had the balloons on either side of his head and asked her if she liked his Mickey Mouse impression. She must have done as they became inseparable. They had their first proper date a few weeks later when Rhys flew Alice out to New York to visit him.

Not to be outdone, Lucy found herself in the company of Andy, a very good family friend. They both realised that they lived in London and the romance continued when they got back.

Our laidback wedding became the catalyst for two more successful marriages.

I had organised a ceilidh band from Durham University to come and play for us. The last thing we wanted was a loud, annoying disco. I always loved a good ceilidh and I knew it would appeal to young and old alike and people wouldn't have to just sit around and make polite conversation if they didn't want to.

We had our very first, and to this day, last, dance together at everyone's insistence. The fiddler played a lively tune and we had to stomp around the floor in each other's arms for an excruciating minute. Eventually, people relented and joined us on the dancefloor. We were both much happier not being under the microscope. The ceilidh was a great success and I joined in the reels and flings despite my dress.

David stood on the side-lines chatting to family, friends and work colleagues, a pint in hand. I was aware that this wasn't the norm for the bride and groom at a wedding, but it was never meant to be a normal wedding. I had never set out to change him. I can't deny I would have liked him to join in but my intuition told me he wasn't comfortable in that kind of public display and I knew in my heart of hearts that that wouldn't change.

People ask me when I first knew David had Asperger's. I think I always knew; I just didn't know it had a name.

I Didn't Sign up for This

We had a quiet honeymoon in Ireland. I had wanted to go to Bali as I had never been anywhere hot and exotic but David told me his skin was too sensitive and he didn't like the heat. He was well travelled so that kind of holiday just didn't appeal to him at all. As my first real compromise, I agreed to go to Ireland in October.

I think I had him on a pedestal a lot of the time and respected what he said. He always seemed so confident about everything. He always had an answer and a solution. It hadn't felt right to insist on going to a hot country when he didn't want to.

It rained.

I also had the worst hangover. I had barely eaten on our wedding day due to nerves and then David had plied me with gin and tonic in the car. The drinks hadn't stopped flowing all day until we left for the hotel later that night.

For fun, we had booked a themed room in the Marriott hotel which I had really been looking forward to. By the time we arrived I was so tired that when the staff sheepishly informed us they had double booked our room because a flight had been delayed I was past caring. David looked to me to decide about whether we should insist or whether we should just accept a cheaper room. I was standing there in the reception, still in my wedding dress and just wanted to go to bed. I was annoyed that he couldn't just take control of the situation.

Two weeks away was too long. Though Ireland was lovely, David seemed very distant at times. We ran out of things to say to each other. He didn't ever want to do anything

61

adventurous. We would drive somewhere nice but then he seemed to consider we had done the place when we had hardly left the car. On the other hand, the weather was hardly on our side. I spent quite a lot of time doing my maths homework and revision as I was retaking my GCSE in the hope of becoming an English teacher in the future.

I liked Dublin, what little we saw of it. David was pretty much only happy if we went to places where we could eat. He wasn't interested in walking or museums or night clubs.

We were very amused by Irish culture. We always knew that the Irish like potatoes and indeed I am an eighth Irish and love my potatoes but not quite to the same extent. On an evening in the hotels we would be served by very friendly staff who would come around with platters of food. I happily accepted some roast potatoes from. Then the server would come back with more potatoes, I was a bit confused at first and pointed out I had potatoes but he assured me that I would want these as these were boiled and buttered potatoes. So, I slightly bemusedly accepted the boiled potatoes onto my plate when he came back a third time offering me mashed potatoes. This time I didn't' argue as it seemed rather rude! There was barely any room on my plate for any greens!

Maybe David had chosen Ireland because it was the closest foreign country to Britain and he wouldn't have any difficulty with the culture. We had more difficulty than expected. David after all likes to abide by the rules and the Irish, not so much. We bought a map to help us navigate the countryside but we soon realised that there were a lot of roads missing from it. So, we bought another map which also had completely different missing roads on it. We ended up having to use two maps at the same time to find our way from place to place. I'm not a bad navigator thankfully. Sometimes we would let the atmosphere go to our heads and just wing it and not use maps at all!

There didn't seem to be any such thing as a motorway or dual carriageway in Ireland or at least not on the routes we ended up taking. We soon noticed that if some cars wanted to drive at a leisurely pace that they would just drive half way on the hard shoulder and half way on the road to enable other drivers to get passed. This blew David's mind for a while but he likes to do as the locals do so he too started to do this.

Doubts

After a few days, I started to wonder if I had done the right thing in marrying David. He was not the sparkling man he had been on our wedding day. It was as if he had put on an act and was now all burned out. There was nothing left over for me. I realise now that for David, the end result had been the wedding and proving he could get a wife. For me, the wedding was the start of the rest of our life together. He stopped trying almost as soon as I had signed the contract. I'm not sure most brides are relieved when their honeymoon is over. I wanted to get home and speak to other people as David was severely lacking in conversation. Perhaps he was already starting to feel out of his depth.

We managed to explore Blarney Castle but we only watched other people attempt to kiss the Blarney Stone. We wandered aimlessly in the damp castle grounds for a bit before returning to the hotel via a rather circuitous route. Getting lost tended to be the highlight of our days. We visited an old school friend of mine who was doing her medical residency in Cork and David who had only met her briefly at the wedding was on his best behaviour for her. It was so lovely to get to talk to someone else! I think even David was keen to see Liz, even though he hardly knew her. We apparently drank the Jury's hotel in Cork out of Bombay Sapphire and we had to resort to the Cork Dry Gin. It was rough stuff, but needs must!

At long last, the time came to make our way home and we returned for one last night in Dublin. We visited the same places we went before and felt quite at home before returning to the airport.

On the return flight, with Aer Lingus of course, the captain announced that there was a problem with the engines and that we were not to be concerned but we would be returning to Dublin airport. Despite his laidback accent and approach to the situation there was a terrified silence from all passengers until we landed safely, at which point one man ran at lightning speed from the back of the plane and locked himself in the toilet.

Married Life

When we eventually got home, our little house suddenly felt quite small. Despite not having asked for presents, our wedding guests had still been generous and our little two up, two down, house couldn't really cope with it. I wanted to move nearer my family as I didn't really like where the house was situated, right next to the Team Valley Industrial Estate. It wasn't on any convenient bus routes and a long way from any Metro or train stations and I didn't drive.

This was the source of our first real argument. I don't think it had ever occurred to David that marrying me would bring change. I had ambitions and, as much as his little house was very nice, I had obviously never been part of the decision to buy it and I wanted us to purchase something together, to make our stamp on our marriage. It still felt like I was living in David's house that he had bought with his mother's help rather than our home. Also, I wasn't on the mortgage.

Of course, this meant extra expense and David started to freak out about the thought of a larger mortgage, even though I was now bringing in money too. It was the first time I had seen him lose his temper with me and become irrational about money. I couldn't understand his reluctance. It took me a while to persuade him that we needed to move, but eventually even he could see that we had outgrown his little abode. We put the house on the market and started looking around for houses nearer to his work and my parents.

He didn't seem to have any idea what he wanted but soon my ideas became his own. I was brought up in Edwardian or Victorian period homes and I loved the history and space they provided. Whitley Bay had a lot of Victorian terraced houses but David wasn't keen on ones that needed work and we couldn't afford the ones that were already done up. Every time we found a house we both liked someone would beat us to it.

After a few months of searching and disappointment, I suggested that we look at new build homes. To our surprise we found a lovely show home not far from Whitley Bay with very affordable, good sized houses on them. We sold our little house and put a deposit down on the three-bedroom detached in West Allotment. We had to wait several months for it to be built, so we had to move in with my parents.

David spent longer and longer at work and when he was in the house he would spend most of it in our room. He was anxious and on edge and uncomfortable living in someone else's house. It was such a contrast to see as I was used to him being so confident and reliable all the time. Life is full of little disappointments and I am used to them. It makes the successes that much better but David couldn't cope with the uncertainty of buying houses. I was generally just an optimistic person who expected everything to work out in time.

I started working for the council again but this time I was sent to a social services office in in the west end of Newcastle, not known for being salubrious. It was a very different environment to gas servicing and housing, dealing with the public face to face, one that was always seemed to be on the defensive. The clients were rude and aggressive and seemingly unappreciative of any help. One young mum came in to use our 'phones to sort her benefits out and she let her two toddlers run riot around the waiting area. The two-year-old climbed unsupervised onto a seat and then tried to get out of an open window. We were on the first floor. I dived across the room and grabbed the child to stop it falling to its death and he told me to, "Fuck off!"

I made some good friends who considered me to be an expert with computers. Some employees had never used a Windows system before or even a mouse. One of my most persistently inept colleagues was Steve, bearded, laid back social worker. After a few weeks, I was warned by Kim in admin that there were mutterings in the next-door office about my relationship with Steve. I was a bit surprised as I didn't think I had a 'relationship' with Steve. I would chat and have a laugh with him but that was all.

One Monday morning after an office night out, I was in the store cupboard next to the welfare rights office. I heard one of the women talk about "that temp who was all over the men on Friday night". My blood ran cold and I tried to remember what I had done that was so terrible on Friday. I had spent most of the evening talking to Steve and Phil but they were just mates and we had had a good laugh. It wasn't until I recounted this to Kim that she informed me that this woman had quite the thing for Steve and was jealous me. Kim also pointed out that Steve did seem to like me a lot.

He did seem rather protective of me. He knew I had been married just a few months and had apparently voiced concerns about the way David treated me. This echoed uncomfortably in my own mind but which I swiftly buried.

Whilst we stayed with my parents it coincided with them selling Alma Place. They had decided to buy a four-bed terrace in Whitley Bay to be in the school catchment area for my sister. The sale went through very quickly so we moved in with them briefly in and then had to help them pack and we moved again. All very confusing for our poor little spaniel.

Thankfully, we only had to stay in Whitley Bay with my parents for another month before our house was ready. As our furniture was in storage, we only had a mattress when we moved in. We couldn't wait another day to have our own home again.

Child Protection

Shortly after, I was moved from the west of Newcastle to the east, back to Byker to work as an assistant for the Registrar in the Child Protection Unit there. It was a promotion and a pay rise which I was grateful for but the atmosphere was completely different. There was none of the same camaraderie. At first, I didn't like the job. The woman I was working with complained about everything and a lot of the work was repetitive but worse, the subject matter was harrowing. The area was very dodgy and I didn't enjoy walking up to the Metro Station through the infamous Byker Wall. To cap it all, Maureen, the Registrar had a terrible relationship with the minute takers in the office down the corridor. The atmosphere was tense and bitchy.

I did my best to ignore it all, but a few weeks in, Maureen declared she was going off sick. She spent the rest of the day training me to do her job. This was two levels above my own and then she went home early and never came back. I had been dropped in the deep end but suddenly I had responsibility and was the only person capable of doing that job. I thrived. I had to deal with all the social workers in the whole of Newcastle who needed information on the 'At Risk' or 'Looked After Children'. I would regularly be contacted by concerned doctors at regional hospitals, regarding patients and I was in regular contact with the police. I was on first name terms with many of them.

Just before Christmas I was reading through some minutes of a child protection case, it was my responsibility to do this most days, when I started to feel quite tearful. This wasn't me at all, though the information I was reading held some horrific information, it was no worse than other ones I have previously checked through and filed. I started to wonder if I was pregnant.

Baby

David and I hadn't discussed having children but we were no longer taking any precautions. We hadn't openly admitted we did want a baby but I think with settling down into our lovely new home we had slowly realised that this was what we wanted. Or at least what I wanted.

On my way home that night I bought a pregnancy testing kit. After waiting for three agonising minutes, I dared to have a peek at the stick. At first, I didn't think there was anything there but when I held it up to the light there was the faintest silvery line. Did this mean I was pregnant or not? The instructions implied that I was. I had to wait until David came home that evening and ask him what he thought. He wasn't sure either.

I made an appointment with my GP and he asked me to give a urine sample. Dr Tharakan blandly informed me that if there was a line on the kit, however faint, then I was pregnant. He flippantly mentioned if their test came back negative, they would contact me. In the meantime, he gave me a prescription for folic acid, told me I'd start to feel tired and that the midwife would be in touch.

Immediately I felt very pregnant and very tired. When I got home in the evenings I would have a kip on the sofa before David got home. I couldn't stand the smell of alcohol and no longer had any desire for Chinese and Indian takeaways. In fact, many ordinary smells made me want to vomit, though I never did.

When I was twelve weeks pregnant I rang the surgery to find out when the midwife was going to be in contact with me. The receptionist sounded astounded and said "Oh, Mrs Rowlands, we couldn't find your file to contact you. You're not pregnant!"

I sat at my desk staring into space. I had already told my parents and close friends. I didn't believe it. I was sure I was pregnant. I couldn't concentrate on work and left early. I went straight in to town, bought another test in Boots and went to Bainbridge's toilets. I had bought a different kit this time. Almost immediately a bright pink line appeared on the stick. This time, I was definitely pregnant. I was over the moon and very much relieved.

I walked through the baby department on cloud nine and made my first purchase of a dog shaped, fluffy rug for the baby's bedroom.

I should have changed my GP at that point but there weren't any sensible options. Once I informed them I most definitely was pregnant they immediately sent the midwife on a home visit. Maggie was lovely and reassuring. She found the baby's heartbeat straight away, so that there was no doubt. That was the strangest feeling and confirmed I was going to be a mum.

David was wonderfully caring and supportive throughout my whole pregnancy. As well as full time work I had decided in the September to better myself and try yet again to gain a maths GCSE. On Monday evenings, I would go to college and sit with a load of uninterested teenagers. I had more motivation than they had to pass the exam but as my pregnancy progressed, I became increasingly more exhausted and sometimes didn't make it to the classes.

David never teased me about not having my maths. I was always embarrassed and ashamed that I had never passed. I was the black sheep of the family as everyone else just sailed through their maths exams and went on to do 'A' level too. My intention was to do a PGCE and teach English but to my frustration I couldn't get on the course without GCSE maths.

When I struggled, David was always helpful, supportive and patient and explained things so clearly. When I was a child and it became obvious I didn't have a natural aptitude for numbers, my dad would insist on tutoring me. This always ended in disaster. He was very impatient and didn't explain things at my level. He made me very nervous as I didn't want to let him down. To make matters worse, I developed a nervous laugh, which I realise now was hysteria. That made my dad even more cross. It always ended up with at least one of us shouting and me in tears. David on the other hand, explained things in a way that made sense and wasn't at all patronising. The only problem I had was retaining the information.

He was always willing to help and support me in whatever I was doing and never looked down on any of the jobs I did. I was contacted by the Director of children's services office. They made it clear they needed information and it was a priority. I was asked to provide some statistics of children on the register. Thankfully, with a few 'phone calls to David at work, I could persuade the complicated database to give up a correct answer by the end of the day. That evening we were watching the local news when my statistics were announced and had been turned into a lovely graphic. I'm so glad I hadn't known beforehand that my information was going to be made public.

The database I had to cope with was extremely old but had recently been adapted to a Windows system and the councils' IT department had grafted Windows Access on to it to make it easier to use. I had used Windows systems for years and different databases at university. I had also used Excel quite a lot but I had never been given a chance to use Access. I assumed it worked just like the others.

I was so wrong.

One memorable day I was struggling to get some statistics about boys on the register and decided the easiest way would be to do a cut and paste. I got my results and passed the information on. It was only later when I was inputting additional information, that I noticed that my numbers had decreased dramatically. Now I know that when you cut and paste in Microsoft Access, you literally delete the original information from the database. I had just removed half the children from the child protection register and had no way to fix it. That was another 'blood runs cold' moment.

I rang David in a panic and confessed what I had done, thankful that I worked in an office by myself. He patiently explained my mistake and offered to come and fix it but I thought that would look too suspicious. Thankfully, as I had been taught by Maureen my predecessor, the last thing I did before leaving every night was set up the back-up tape. I knew I could not restore the backup myself and would have to ring the IT helpline in the Civic Centre. David told me that whatever I did, not to set the backup running that night or I would lose all the girls from the system forever. I rang the IT department and they confirmed this saying that they would come as quickly as possible but it would probably be a couple of days.

They were possibly the longest two days of my life. I didn't tell my boss Rick, as I didn't want to appear a complete idiot but also, he was such a lovely guy I didn't want to panic him. At the end of the day, I was just a temp and could walk away if I wanted to. Every time someone came into my office and asked me for information I would pray it wouldn't be about the girls I had deleted. Somehow, I got away with it and the sight of the IT team coming to restore everything was the biggest relief ever. I felt that I could breathe again. I did confess to Rick what I had done but only after the event. He did admit he was grateful I had sorted it out myself as he was already stressed with his workload.

That summer we had good weather and many sunny days with high temperatures. This was lovely apart from the fact I was heavily pregnant and working in an office with bars on the windows that did not open. I was sweltering and the electric fan I had brought in, didn't seem to make much difference. By the end of June, I couldn't find any decent shoes to fit me, so I had to resort to wearing Velcro walking sandals over my sausage feet. I was past the point of caring how I looked. I had decided to go on maternity leave a month before the baby was due. I was having real difficulty getting up and down when opening the filing cabinets, most of the files I needed seemed to always be in the bottom drawer.

We attended a couple of antenatal classes at the local hospital and were shown around the wards and told what to expect. The classes were quite fun and I remember one girl, who stood out because of her southern accent who asked lots of questions. She was called Sam and was due a month before me.

Despite David noticing my growing bump and how tired I was, I'm not sure the baby became a reality to him, even with the scans. Cuddled up in bed one night, the baby started kicking him in the back. He was amazed by this development and began taking more of an interest in his child after that. He helped me decorate the second bedroom in blue and he drilled and put up shelving in there too. I remember sitting watching him noisily drilling and the baby reacting and kicking violently to the loud sound.

I spent the first week of my maternity leave worrying about my replacement at work and how she was coping and how she was coping and then I completely forgot about it. We had a solar eclipse in August 1999 and I remember sitting at home by myself, watching the sky slowly and eerily darken whilst listening to the commentary on the BBC News. David was at work. My only caller that week was the health visitor Corinne, who came for a home visit.

Having just spent the last year working deep within child protection and spending much of my time reading health visitors reports on the state of the homes they visited, I was completely paranoid about her visit. I must have spent many hours scrubbing and cleaning the whole house in case she considered my house filthy and therefore I would not be considered a good mother. I was only too aware of how many babies were removed from their mother's arms and placed in care in Newcastle. Rationality had nothing to do with it. We had a beautiful, brand new house on a lovely estate and the coming baby would obviously want for nothing. This did not stop me from being nervous when I first met Corinne but she was lovely and we both relaxed when she found out about my job.

Parenthood

James was due on 21st August 1999 but everyone had warned me he wouldn't arrive on his due date. About midnight, I woke with a strong desire to get to the toilet. I didn't make it; my waters broke on the bathroom floor. David was fast asleep but I left him while I cleaned up. After a while my contractions started and I decided I had better wake David him. I told him as gently as possible, so as not to panic him, that I thought I was in labour. He leapt out of bed but then didn't know what to do. Once he'd woken up properly, he rang the maternity department and answering their questions, arranged for us to come in.

It was a long night but I do remember David being wonderful and supportive the whole time. My usual midwife had advised on pain medication and she suggested for me to have Diamorphine if I felt I needed it. I was determined to last as long as possible without any medication but after a few tiring hours of little progress and a lot of pain, I asked the midwife, quite stroppily if I remember rightly, when I was going to get some pain relief.

The sensation of first the needle and then the warm, calming sensation spreading from my hip was instant. I had an image in my head of the drug travelling in blue streaks through the veins in my body. I knew immediately why heroin was addictive. I have no idea whether anyone else would visualise it like that. I have never asked. I do wonder if I do have mild synaesthesia, having watched a documentary on the subject, certain aspects made sense to me. I associate colours with different thoughts, sensations and people's names. It enables me to have strong memories about certain events. This I remember particularly well but I don't remember much about the labour after I took it.

In hindsight, I wished I hadn't listened to Maggie, as after a while I couldn't feel my contractions at all and I just had to guess when to push. James was born just before two in the afternoon. I was exhausted. He cried when he came out and pooed meconium all over me. Apparently, this is a sign of distress but no one informed me of that. I'd secretly wanted a little girl but the moment they told me it was a boy it didn't matter and I felt a fierce protectiveness and love for him.

When I got to hold James, he just lay there looking at me with his blue eyes. He was very quiet. I don't remember much about what David was up to. I think he must have been exhausted too. After they delivered my placenta we were left alone but suddenly there was a massive gush of blood which covered the bed and splashed onto the floor. Apparently, I had had a blood clot behind the placenta. They seemed to think this was nothing to worry about.

I was horrified by the amount I bled afterwards but assumed it was perfectly normal. I was shunted on to a ward and left with my baby. There were six beds on the ward, all full and two were Caesareans. No one seemed to speak to anyone. Perhaps they were all traumatised too.

I would get quite stressed if James cried as I felt we were disturbing everyone else's sleep. I tried to feed him myself but he wasn't having it. I asked a midwife for help but she was very dismissive, saying she was at the end of her shift and would ask someone else to come. They never did.

At visiting time, David's parents turned up first. Linda burst into tears the moment she saw James, declaring,

"He's just like David!".

How right she was, in more ways than one. He did indeed
look like his dad, the early form of a DNA test kicking in,
but these days he looks just like me.

The following day I was still struggling to feed James. David
had drawn the curtain around the bed and I was trying to get
James to take an interest. My mum suddenly popped her
head through the curtain. She explained that she had had an
oncology appointment and thought she'd just pop in to see
us. I was really pleased to see her, as who better to help than
my mum who'd breastfed all four of us. Yet, before I could
react, David had grabbed her by the shoulders and
frogmarched her out. I remember sitting there in shock, not
knowing what to say about the way he had not only
dismissed my mum but actually manhandled her. I felt
totally helpless and lost and awful for my mum.

To top it all, an auxiliary kept coming around with a formula
milk round, in what seemed like every twenty minutes,
shouting,

"SMA! Cow and Gate!"

like a fishwife selling her wares. I turned her down every
time, even though I was still struggling to feed James and
never got any help before were discharged.

Before coming to hospital, I had packed my bag in advance
as we had been advised. For some reason, which escapes me
now, I had omitted to put in clothes for myself for leaving
hospital. I had to ask David to pick up a jumper and a pair
of trousers for me. Now with an extra eighteen years'
experience, I know never to give him this kind of
responsibility. It sends his head into a spin. I should at least
have been more specific. He turned up and presented me

with one of my favourite jumpers and trousers which I obviously hadn't worn for a while. However, I would never have worn them together. The trousers were brown and yellow checked (I called them my Rupert Bear trousers) and the jumper was bright blue and green striped. He couldn't understand why I burst out laughing at his choice.

We carried James out and spent an eternity fitting him into his enormous, car seat. David had not worked out how it went in the car before coming to get us. This was in the days before baby seats could be popped in and out with Isofix. The drive home was not very far but took an eternity. David drove the car like an old man. The roundabout directly outside the hospital suddenly became a death trap to him and he ended up giving way to every car approaching. Eventually when the coast was clear, he trickled on to it. This was the guy who I was more used to rallying his car at every opportunity. We eventually trundled up to our house and got James out. I popped him into his bouncer and he fell asleep. We looked at each other. What do we do now?

Because of the experience I had had with my little sister, I had expected that motherhood would be difficult, but I was confident I would cope. I was wrong. I still had trouble feeding James. My visiting midwife was full of advice but still he always seemed to be hungry and he just cried the whole time. I was in agony with my boobs and I tried every position and every form of protection for them, cabbage leaves, plastic nipples, you name it. I was determined to give my son the best.

Over the August bank holiday when James was just over a week old, my usual midwife was away. The locum was horrified when she saw James. She said he was starving and had a 'dry cry'. I felt terrible. I explained to her how I'd tried everything with him and how he just wouldn't feed. She whipped out a bottle from her bag and he gulped it down. I felt so guilty. She weighed him for me and he had lost nearly 3lbs. She announced he was dehydrated and immediately arranged for him to go back into hospital.

We ended up on the children's ward with a lot of doctors and nurses surrounding him on the stark bed, while James cried. I couldn't get near him. I tried to explain I'd spent the last ten days trying to feed him. David told the staff we were failures as parents. I couldn't believe he had said that. I had tried everything I could with my baby until I was utterly exhausted. I agreed to stop trying to breast feed him and give him formula which every magazine article I had read in my pregnancy had been strongly against.

We stayed in hospital for a few days until he started to put weight on and began to look like a healthy baby again. I can't look at the photos I have of him during that time, as now I can see he's terribly thin for a new born baby. How did I not see it?

Looking back now, I realise I'd taken to heart the 'breast is best' campaign and I was let down by the hospital staff. Also, it turned out I was very anaemic and exhausted which had been missed, due to the blood clot perhaps? So, I think it was no wonder I didn't have enough milk for him. I don't remember much about what David did but I think he just left it all to me. He didn't know what to do, so didn't do anything.

I found out recently, seventeen years down the line that David thought I had post-natal depression. I distinctly remember crying on day four, when my milk came in. I was sitting on the bed crying for absolutely no reason. If he truly thought I had post-natal depression, why didn't he talk to me about it or share his concerns with the midwife? I know for a fact I was just going through the normal feelings of any new mother but he wasn't used to seeing me so emotional and not in control.

David had taken time off while James was born but soon went back to work. I didn't really know anyone in the area other than my parents who lived about five miles away. I didn't drive, so if I wanted to see them I either had to get a couple of buses or walk a mile or more to the nearest Metro station. Until I established a routine with James it was hard to get out of the house. I rediscovered day time television.

During those early days of motherhood, I didn't have the time or the energy to be lonely. I was too busy being a new mum and I'd always known David would only be around in the evenings. I had hoped he would be home a little sooner. I had had fantasies of him coming home, cooing over his son and wanting to bathe him and put him to bed every night. One night I did suggest that he bath James when he got home. He came home in reasonable time and was certainly present in the bathroom whilst his child was washed, but after that he must have thought he'd done his bit.

Stifled Emotion

David's father had been very ill for as long as I had known him. He was a very thin man with Type 1 diabetes and looked far older than his 57 years. I had always liked Jimmy despite the fact he was gruff and a man of few words. Those words were also relayed in a thick Northumbrian accent, laced with many colloquialisms and I had found it hard to understand him at first. But I soon realised beneath the tough exterior was a man who dearly loved and admired his children. Jimmy had been very keen for James to be born and had made it to the hospital to see him but had unfortunately ended up back in hospital himself since then. We already knew he had heart failure but I didn't really know what that meant. Jane, his daughter who was a junior doctor at the time, knew exactly what it meant and I suspect David did too, though he never talked about it.

After Jimmy got very ill, David didn't go and see his father in hospital anymore. He told me he hated hospitals. Instead, his sister visited from Liverpool regularly and spent a lot of time with Linda at her father's bedside. It soon became apparent to me, even through my exhaustion with the baby, that all was not looking good. Linda came and stayed the night at our house as it was too far to go back to Kielder. There was a lot of coming and going in the middle of the night, backwards and forth to the hospital. Eventually Jane and Linda retuned saying that Jimmy had gone. They were both in tears but holding each other together. David rushed around looking after them as if it didn't affect him. I never saw him cry.

David wrote a touching eulogy for his father which he stood up and read out in a very calm and composed manner at the funeral. I was very proud of him but also very concerned that he hadn't shown anything more than a little sadness. I asked him directly if he had cried at all and he told me he had while writing the eulogy. I'm not sure I believed him. I was pretty sure he was telling me that to make himself seem normal.

Sleep Deprivation

Not long after James was born, Sam from my antenatal group rang for a chat. We had met up once before the babies were born and I had spoken to her after her son had been born in the July, but we hadn't really had a chance to catch up since. At the time, I didn't know much about her, just that like me, she wasn't local either. I didn't realise that she was probably feeling lonely too.

Sam could drive and on the odd occasion when she had the car she would come over to see me. It wasn't far by car, but to get from my house to her house by public transport was a ninety-minute journey. We would just sit and chat for hours, nursing our baby boys. I think we were a lifeline to each other without realising it.

I was still up with James every night. I never got more than an hour or two of sleep at a time. He was such a clingy baby and did not like to be left at all. After three months, I thought it was time that he went in his own room, which I'm sure did not help James at all, even though it was the done thing. I never expected David to get up to James as after all he was the one that had to go to work every day. I would spend hours at night pacing, jiggling, singing and feeding; trying to get James to sleep. When I would put him in his cot he would grab my fingers and not let go. I would sit on the floor for ages until he fell asleep and I could eventually ease my fingers out from his tiny, vice-like grip.

David in the meantime would be downstairs watching TV, on the computer or fast asleep.

I would regularly walk the mile to the local clinic and meet up with other mums there, though I never succeeded in making any close friendships. The main topics were sleep, colic and for those working mums; the stress of trying to get their baby off the breast and to accept a bottle, in time for them to return to work. Most of them were planning to return after three months. Nowadays, new mothers seem to get a lot more time off, up to a year. I used to secretly resent the mums who would casually drop into conversations,

"Oh, he slept through again last night," or complain they'd only had eight hours sleep. I couldn't even dream of having that much sleep.

I woke with a jolt one morning, sometime after David had left for work. I had been vaguely aware that he had left but hadn't got up to see him off. I suddenly realised that James had not screamed for me to get him. This was very unusual. I lay in bed wondering what to do, listening in case he was making any noise at all. He was not a child that played and gurgled in his cot.

In the end, I couldn't bear it anymore and tiptoed across the landing, avoiding the squeaky floorboards, and listened outside his door. No sound at all. I wondered whether I should go in and check to see if he was okay. I seriously pondered on this but I didn't want to waste this precious time by disturbing him. Was this the start of a new routine? I shouldn't jeopardise it if it was. Or the other dark thought that was niggling me and had made me get up in the first place, was what if he was dead? I seriously considered this too. He had never slept this long. It was unnatural. In my sleep-deprived state, I concluded that if he was still asleep I should leave him and if he was dead, there was nothing I could do. I reasoned he would have been dead a long time.

After further deliberation, I decided I needed sleep more. I went back to bed. It wasn't long before I was woken back up by a familiar and hungry scream from my healthy, wide awake son.

When James was six months old, I had to unexpectedly go back to work. David had not been looking after the car and the engine had packed in. It cost £2000 to repair. I have no idea why David ignored all the warning signs, being an engineer and having worked in his parents' garage for years, he must have known. Because we had this bill that we couldn't afford, within the week I had contacted the council again, got a job back in housing and found a local child minder.

Part of me was actually excited at the prospect of going back to work and dealing with people again.

I hated the job.

I was administrative assistant to the director of housing's PA. Chrissie was a big woman in all senses of the word and she was a bitch. She didn't like me from the off, despite the fact she had interviewed me. I don't think she liked the fact that I was happily married and had previously had a better job and was better educated than her. Which is not the kind of thing I would ever rub in someone's face but she had read my application form.

I started to get migraines which I put down to being overly tired. One day I went into the office and sat at my computer. I could barely see the screen. It seemed to be covered in lots of black dots. I had to make my excuses and go home. I took a week off work until my vision improved. That didn't go down well.

I did partly enjoy returning to work just to get dressed smartly and to be treated as someone with a purpose. Though more than once when I entered the Housing floor at the Civic Centre, I would be stopped by an amused colleague who would wipe the baby sick off the back of my jacket.

I asked for a day off to take James to a clinic appointment which was reluctantly given. In the afternoon, I took him to town and thought I would call in at work with James. Along the corridor colleagues stopped me to admire and talk to my happy, smiling, blonde haired, blue eyed boy. We popped into my office to see Chrissie and I sat James on her desk. She looked horrified.

"This is *your* baby?" she asked in surprise. She obviously assumed I would produce some ugly monster. She never said a civil word to me again.

One weekend I complained to David how tired I was because James still wasn't sleeping and of course I was now working full-time as well. He decided the answer was for him to move into the spare bedroom. In that one statement, I felt utterly abandoned and let down. It was not the answer I was looking for! In fact, I don't think I was looking for an answer other than a chance to moan. I have since learned not to expect that kind of rhetorical support. In fact, I have learned there is no such thing as a rhetorical conversation in my household.

I was gutted by his reaction as it implied that he didn't want to share a room with me. Obviously, my getting up and down all night with James crying was inconveniencing him. I completely lost my temper with him. I shouted,

"If that's what you want, you can move in there now!"

I handed him the baby and started removing David's clothes from the matching dressing room wardrobes. I started flinging them into the spare room with great ferocity. David followed me back and fore demanding to know what I was doing.

That wasn't good enough for me. I needed to let my feelings be heard for a change. He'd always made a point of turning the computer off in the spare room which doubled as a study because of the whirring fan, when people stayed. I announced that he couldn't possibly sleep with the computer in there and that it would have to go downstairs. I started manically pulling out cables left, right and centre. David was sitting in shock on the sofa bed holding a bawling James in his arms. Neither of them had ever seen me react like this before. I was fuming!

With tears running down his face, David begged me to calm down. He'd never seen me so mad before and he was scared of my reaction. Eventually my temper fizzled out, leaving us both wrung out and with a screaming baby. In a way, it was good for me to let it all out. I tend to just bottle things up, never complain or shrug things off. I did feel bad for David afterwards as he genuinely looked terrified. I think he tiptoed around me for a while after that.

Thankfully, I didn't stay in the housing department for too long but was moved down a floor to children's services where I already knew a lot of people. My vision in my right eye however got much worse. I went to see my GP. I could tell he had absolutely no interest. He shone a torch in the direction of my eye from across the desk. He gave me a prescription for some codeine, despite the fact I had no headache and sent me off to see my optician.

I don't know what the optician was looking for but he seemed to completely miss the fact that I had a blood vessel bursting in my macula. He passed me as fit. By this time, I had little vision in my right eye and would bump into people on the street. Looking back, I can't believe I kept working. I told David that I couldn't see, but her just gave me the silent treatment as if I was doing it deliberately. he never encouraged me to go to the hospital or ask me how I was.

Exhaustion

When James was a year old, we went on holiday to France
with my parents. We squeezed into a little holiday cottage
with them, my thirteen-year-old sister and my good friend
Beckie. James had just started to take his first steps. I have
some lovely photos of him toddling excitedly across the lawn
towards me. Early one morning we were all sitting around
the traditional French kitchen and James was tottering across
the floor towards me when he fell and banged his head.
David was washing dishes at the sink at the time and I was
too far away to catch him. I rushed up to James as he
screamed. David shouted at me, blaming me for James's
tumble. It hadn't been anyone's fault. James was fine, but I
was more upset about being shouted at unnecessarily by
David and for everyone else to witness it. I think my mum
must have had a word with him because later he did come
and apologise, saying he had been scared for James. It's
possibly one of the only times he has ever actually
apologised for doing something wrong.

On the return journey, we got the ferry to Dover and from
there to Cardiff to drop Beckie off and visit old friends.
Later that evening, on the way back to the hotel, I started
feeling strange. I knew I was tired and stressed, because
David had been in a difficult mood all day but I started to
have pins and needles in my hands and my tongue and jaw
became so stiff I could barely move it. I was sitting in the
passenger seat of the car while James slept in the back. I had
been agitated for some time and had anxiously been rubbing
my arms, not knowing what to do. I thought that maybe I
had septicaemia as I had cut my hand on a broken fish tank
in a French restaurant, a few days earlier.

I knew we were on the outskirts of Cardiff and were close to the University Hospital. In fact, I had seen a sign for it on the side of the dual carriageway. When David eventually noticed my distress, he snapped at me,

"What's the matter with you? Do I need to take you to hospital?"

I think he was calling my bluff and expecting me to say No. Normally, I would have, not wanting to cause a fuss, but I felt so ill and thinking I might possibly die replied,

"Yes".

His attitude swiftly turned to panic. He hadn't expected me to agree. Through my haze, I still had to direct him to the Accident and Emergency entrance. I staggered into A & E, while he parked the car and looked after James. I could barely walk. Thankfully, I was seen almost straightaway as the staff must have seen that I was in a terrible state.

They tested my heart and took bloods and then left me in a cubicle for a while, David sat with me looking worried. In the end, they couldn't find anything physically wrong with me, other than my blood results came back with low potassium. They asked me if I'd ever suffered from a panic attack. Why were they asking me this? This wasn't a panic attack. I was going to die!

Thankfully, Beckie was there to look after James who miraculously slept through the whole debacle. While the doctors were giving me all kinds of tests, she later confessed that David had cried on her shoulder, he was so terrified. He hadn't shown any sign of this when he was in the room with me. I suspect his composure was more for the doctor's sake than my own.

After drinking a lot of water and calming down sufficiently, I was sent home. We were meant to stay in a cheap hotel in Cardiff Bay but my aunt Maria insisted that I stay the night with them, regardless of what time it was. It took me forever to calm down and go to sleep. I kept thinking I was going to have another panic attack. I didn't discuss how I felt with David; I didn't want to distress him further.

Back home, I soon decided that I couldn't continue working. My eye sight was so bad, I was still shattered from lack of sleep and I was fragile after the panic attack. I gave the council a month's notice and looked forward to just being a mum again. David did not object.

During our first year with James, I had stayed in regular contact with our health visitor. Corinne was supportive and gave plenty of advice in a non-judgmental way. After my little episode in Cardiff, she came to visit and I discussed James's sleep problem and she formulated a plan. Basically, this was: to make sure he is fed; put him to bed and leave him to cry. He'll soon learn.

We knew it would be hard but were prepared to give it a try. I put him in his cot, well-fed, said goodnight and left him. He immediately started to cry. When I didn't go back, the crying just escalated in volume and urgency. Soon it turned from a noisy, attention seeking cry to a despairing, heart wrenching scream. We hadn't heard this before. We tried to ignore the sound. We cranked up the volume on the television. This, we had been assured, was perfectly normal and he would soon give up and go to sleep. He didn't. The screams became unbearable for us to cope with. I stood at the bottom of the stairs, all my instincts screaming along with him. In the end, it was David who cracked first but I wasn't far behind.

90

I rescued my tiny son from his baby prison. He was gulping and sobbing in absolute terror and misery. This was no annoyed baby who was having a routine enforced on him. I just knew in my heart that we couldn't do it to him.

We felt like failures and I think we did try again a few times but this time I didn't let him cry for so long. I just knew he wasn't the kind of baby that could be left. As a mother of an Asperger child I wish I'd known sooner, but, how could I have known?

At eighteen months, he started to sleep a little longer but he would wake up screaming in terror. Or rather, once I got him out the cot, instead of calming down, he would struggle and scream more. As he got bigger I couldn't cope with him and would have to put him down on the floor where he would bang his head or push me away, screaming and staring blindly in horror. At times like this I felt rejected and useless. One particular episode, I carried him downstairs so as not to disturb David too much but he was thrusting me away and screaming at me. I put him on the living room floor and just sat there in despair as he banged his head off the thick carpet. Part of me felt angry. I was so tired and didn't know what to do. I walked into the kitchen to get away from him. The next moment, he came running in after me shouting "Mummy! Mummy!"

He was so scared. Despite him pushing me away he still needed me. I saw he had a different look in his eyes and that he was now aware of what was going on, whereas moments before, he hadn't. My heart immediately melted for him, and I was full of relief that he had snapped out of it and still needed me. I had never heard of night terrors before but I soon found out that these are waking nightmares. I didn't know it was common in autistic children either.

When James was diagnosed nine years later, I rather belatedly felt justified. I had been right. All the times I had been accused of molly-coddling him by other 'well-meaning' people. I knew I was just giving him what he needed. I always wanted him to be more independent and stand up for himself. At times he could, but I knew that my little boy was different and sensitive. I just didn't know that it was a condition.

Other than the sleep, he was not a difficult baby. He was loving, cuddly and bright. He passed all his milestones and started to show an interest in the world and people around him. I didn't have any concerns about his development at all.

Village Life

We had been at our new home for three years before I had the urge to move again. By this time, David had been headhunted by his previous employers who had founded another company in Northumberland. One of the reasons we had moved to this part of Newcastle was the reasonably short and convenient commute. Now for some time, David had been driving through Newcastle and had a fifty-mile round trip every day. It was costing us a fortune in petrol and as David's hours were already long, I hoped by suggesting we move closer, that we would save money and James and I would see more of his dad.

My financial argument won and we put the house on the market. I started searching in the more rural area. I was not familiar with this part of the north east but David was a local lad and had gone to high school nearby.

I arranged to view a house in the village where the new company was located and James and I got the train there. David's work was a convenient five-minute walk from the little village station. Pushing James in his Maclaren up the hill, several people smiled and said "Hello" to me. I knew then that I wanted to live in such a friendly place. The house we viewed was smaller and more expensive than our current one but we knew it was the right thing to do. We offered the asking price and arrived in May 2001, when James was 21 months old.

For a while, David seemed less stressed as we settled into village life. Instead of a long drive he had a five-minute walk through a pretty village to get to work every day. Whenever he found the time to look out of the windows, he could enjoy far-reaching views. He even lost a little weight with the additional exercise.

People soon found out he had skills and was asked to help set up the newly-founded computer club. He enjoyed giving up part of his evenings and Saturday to teach silver surfers the wonders of the internet. I started attending the parish church and was immediately roped in to help with the crèche. This was where I met Charlotte who had a son, just a little younger than James. After our initial shyness, we clicked. She told me about the toddler group and I would see her there or we would bump into each other around the village.

Bobby, the village shop keeper, asked me if I could sing. When I confessed I had sung in the church choir in Cardiff, he recruited me to the Choral Society. It was starting again in September and they were performing Handel's *Messiah*. I hadn't sung any Choral music since I was seventeen but had performed the Messiah a few times in my youth.

I walked in to the Parish Hall on the first Monday night, feeling apprehensive but everyone was very welcoming. I did notice that I was younger than everyone else by at least 20 years. Yet, when we started singing the Hallelujah chorus as a warm up, I got such a buzz from being part of a choir again. I knew I'd made the right decision.

Monday evenings became my time where I could get out of the house, away from domestic demands and release some stress and be myself. It was hard to settle James in bed by 7.30 pm but I just had to trust that David would learn to deal with him.

For the Christmas concert, each choir member was asked to bring along six mince pies for the interval. This being my first time, I didn't want to just buy a box from Tesco. I thought it would be best to bake them myself.

I put my music on to sing along to and made sure James was occupied watching *Toy Story* for the umpteenth time and set about making pastry and buttering baking trays. I was feeling nervous about that evening's performance and anxiety can make me a bit short-tempered. I was also suffering from severe lack of sleep as James was still not sleeping through the night. Sometimes, during a rehearsal, I would momentarily phase out and then feel my body lurch, bringing me back into the room. The intense, two-hour rehearsals made my Mondays longer, but so worthwhile.

David attempted to make conversation with me but as I'm not a natural baker, I was trying to concentrate on what I was doing and not paying him much attention. He became very agitated and starting shouting at me and I reciprocated. He got angry as I was giving the task more attention than I was giving him. He stormed out of the kitchen, shouting something about this would get my attention.

The next thing I knew he was violently kicking the electrical cabinet in the hallway and deliberately smashing the electricity meter. The electricity went off and so did my oven. I was so mad with him! He knew how important this concert was to me and he was trashing the house, stopping me from creating the mince pies for that evening!

In those days it was best not to get me riled. I wouldn't back down.

I let him know in no uncertain terms what I thought of his actions and then went to assess the damage in the hall. I needed to get the oven back on. David was sitting on the stairs, still ranting at me, whilst I went into the cupboard to see covers wrenched off and cracked plastic. He told me not to touch it and I ignored him. The angrier he got, the more I wanted to defy him. I could tell by now that despite the situation looking bad, he hadn't done any real damage. He had knocked and broken the cover off and kicked some switches to the off position. All I needed to do was switch them back on again.

I reached towards the meter and he screamed in terror as he thought I was about to electrocute myself. I had no sympathy for him at this point at and simply ignored him. I switched the meter back on and went back to making my pies. My heart was racing but I was so angry with him. I couldn't believe how extreme his behaviour had been over something so inconsequential.

In writing this I have noticed a pattern. Every time I have a performance, or at least one that he attends, he has a meltdown and makes things very difficult for me in some way. The amount of times I have felt upset by my husband's behaviour, rather than having healthy performance nerves like everyone else! I have been humiliated in front of choir members by his tantrums and forced to conceal my hurt and all this before going out to perform difficult pieces of music in front of a paying audience.

David did come to my first performance but afterwards, when I asked him what he thought, he replied "well it wasn't very rock and roll". It was years before I invited him to another concert.

We soon discovered however, that we did not enjoy living in a semi-detached house with paper thin walls. James would have night terrors on a regular basis and it would take me ages to calm him down. The neighbour complained about the dog howling when I was out and James crying when we were in. Things became tense and I felt we couldn't do anything without the neighbours listening and watching. David and I couldn't even have a satisfactory argument.

When we initially moved to the village it was in the height of the terrible foot and mouth epidemic. It was soon discovered that the source the disease was just a few miles away. All the footpaths had been closed off and there was nowhere to walk the dog. It was already difficult to exercise the dog and look after a toddler. Not surprisingly, the dog became quite hard to handle and on top of the neighbour's complaints I took the sad decision to let him go. I interviewed a few people and Dylan went to live with a couple in Cumbria. I was devastated but relieved. I still feel guilty about having to let him go.

Caring Attitude

I caught the flu. I'd had bad colds before but not like this. I could barely get out of bed. Yet I had to. James needed looking after and David was at work. It didn't occur to him not to go to work. I felt like a terrible mother as I just lay prostrate on the sofa. All I could do was put *Bob the Builder* and *Toy Story* on repeat for James' entertainment. James didn't seem to mind too much. If he could watch the end of *Toy Story* where Woody and Buzz were 'falling with style' on repeat, he was happy.

When David did eventually return from work, I asked him to look after James and crawled to the haven of my bed. I shut the bedroom door as I just couldn't cope with James's demands. Yet very quickly James came and found me. He would hammer on the door crying,

97

"Mummy! Mummy!"

relentlessly. Where was David? Again, I crawled out of bed to let James in for a cuddle. Quite some time later, David found us and seemed annoyed that James was with me. He took James away but it happened a third time. This time I took James back downstairs to find his dad sitting at the computer, oblivious to everything else. He really had no concept of how to entertain his son or that I desperately needed some peace. Thankfully, James was not the kind of child who liked to escape out of the front door at any given opportunity, or he wouldn't have been missed for hours.

A Little Sleep and a Little Surprise

Suddenly and to my great relief, James began to sleep better at night and the extra hours must have gone to my head. When he was two and a half we decided to try for another baby. I didn't feel it was healthy for James to be an only child.

James started at the local pre-school at two and a half years old for just one morning a week. It was traumatic for him. He didn't like going at all. He didn't like joining in and playing games. He didn't like me abandoning him. He didn't like singing. He did like playing trains on the floor or riding the trikes outside. He wasn't any good at anything else though. On the other hand, he wasn't badly behaved but he was very quiet. He didn't say much.

One morning, James was being particularly difficult about going to pre-school. He refused to walk and kept crying. I couldn't' understand what the matter was. David decided to take matters into his own hands and carried James; down the main road, up the hill, over the bridge and into the hall, kicking and screaming all the way. I felt terrible. David was over-reacting but at the same time I was relieved I didn't' have to deal with James. When David got back he was red in the face and sweating. I had hoped that James would have given in to his dad but he hadn't. David had handed him over to the staff and left.

When I picked James up at lunch time, I was taken to one side by the preschool leader. James had eventually calmed down but she was more worried about the state that David had been in. She did suggest that if James really didn't want to go to preschool, he didn't have to go. I think David

99

thought it was our legal obligation when in fact it was just voluntary at that age.

I never knew what to expect when I went to pick James up, but later in the year, the Preschool leader came out to speak to me again: this time she was in tears. I was immediately panicking inside wondering what on earth was going on. Catherine almost hugged me but controlled herself enough to tell me that James had started joining in that day. She had got to see a side of him that we only got to see at home.

In the February, I had a health check with the nurse. When she asked me when my last period was I hesitated and admitted we had just started trying for baby number two. She suggested I do a pregnancy test there and then and to our delight, the line turned blue in front of us. I had become pregnant after just a few weeks. I walked out into the car park with a huge grin on my face and David took one look at me and intuitively for once in his life, remarked,

"You're pregnant!". For a man who can't read facial expressions, he did rather well that day.

In the summer, my eyesight deteriorated again. I had been having driving lessons and was forced to stop for some months because of the spots appearing in my vision. This time I was checked out by the Ophthalmology department in Newcastle but they couldn't find anything obvious. I didn't know whether it was related to the pregnancy or not but again it eventually cleared up. Each time it happened I was scared that this would be it: that I would lose my sight for good. I couldn't articulate this to David and if I didn't mention it, he never thought to ask how I was.

My lasting memory of that pregnancy was that I felt nauseous most of the time. It was hard being a mum of a

two-year-old and feeling tired and nauseous the whole time.
My only break was James attending pre-school one morning
a week and the fact that the Cbeebies channel for toddlers
had started. It was a blessing that he would sit and watch
Bob the Builder quietly while I could just close my eyes for a
few minutes. When he got bored, he would climb onto me
and try peel my eyelids open, asking,

"Mummy, are you there?"

There were days when I would just lie on the settee and
groan, wishing I could be physically sick. I would open the
fridge door when I was hungry, look in and realise I couldn't
possibly eat anything. I lived on oranges and tomatoes. Still,
my skin was great!

Despite this I wasn't unhappy. I was building up a network
of friends in the village. Something I hadn't had since
leaving university. On sunny days, we might sit and chat in
the park whilst our little boys would run around wearing
themselves out.

Samantha's husband came to work at the engineering
business on David's recommendation and they moved
nearby. I inspired Charlotte to join the Choral Society and
when we found out that Samantha could sing, we persuaded
her to join too. All three of us were pregnant with our
second child, though the other two were much further along
than I was. This year, for the Spring Concert, Sam,
Charlotte and I were asked to sing a trio together. We were
all very nervous and practised hard. We did well but the
three of us must have looked a funny sight with our
pregnancy bellies. It was a good bonding moment, for us
and our proud husbands.

It's a good job I was independent and kept myself busy, as much of the time I rarely saw my own husband. He seemed to disappear for twelve hours at a time and would often be busy at the weekends too. The fact that we lived five minutes down the road apparently meant he could stay longer. People were more likely to contact him if he was home and he had the spare keys to the building. If someone needed to gain entry or the fire alarm went off, he was the first port of call. The problem was, he liked to be needed and never said, "No." to a job if asked by work or someone in the village. He couldn't see that we needed him too. We didn't add value to his self-esteem, whereas he felt outsiders would be judging him and therefore he had to do his best for *them*.

It's hard to describe or remember exactly how things changed, I just know that I saw less and less of the David I married and more and more of the angry and irrational husband and father. Yet he was still there for me when it mattered.

Cathryn was born early on a Tuesday morning in November, eight days overdue. We had done things very differently this time. I was terrified of a repeat of the horror of James's birth. We had booked a private room so that I would be able to get some sleep. David's mum drove over from Newcastle to look after James when I knew my contractions had started in earnest. Cathryn was born within four hours of the first strong contraction with only gas and air for pain relief. I was convinced I would have another boy and couldn't believe it when David cried out

"It's a girl!"

It was the first time I'd seen him cry happy tears.

Cathryn was so different from James. I had prepared myself to not be able to feed her, yet she latched on straight away. She was such a happy, contented baby. She would sleep in her little clear plastic crib or if she didn't sleep she would babble away to herself. She was less than a day old and she sounded like she was singing.

Linda brought James, who was now three, to see us in the afternoon after I had had a good sleep. He was happy staying with his grandma which was a relief but he wasn't very interested in his sister. He was much more interested in the wooden train his sister had 'given' to him. I stayed in hospital a couple of days to recover before going home. I didn't want to start out exhausted but I needn't have worried this time.

Cathryn just fitted into our life so easily. I had been practising for our next concert with everyone else but wasn't sure whether I would be able to take part. However, Cathryn was nearly two weeks old and even though she was feeding well, I had experimented with bottles and formula. I hoped that David would be able to bond with her if he was able to help feed her. She was so good I took the risk of going to the concert and singing. Everyone was so surprised to see me. Amazingly, David coped for a couple of hours with a new born baby. I think she slept through most of it but she did take some milk from him. He was rather proud of himself when I returned.

James seemed to accept her quite happily. He didn't seem to resent the attention that she was given. If he was fed and I would answer his questions or help him set up his railway he was happy. He started to pay her attention and use her name in his little squeaky voice, it was so cute.

My brother Nick had bought Cathryn a colourful toy octopus with bells on the end of each tentacle. James thought it was fantastic and went up to her in her bouncy chair saying in his squeaky little voice,

"Look Cathryn! Look what this is!"

He shoved the octopus right into her face and held it there, so she could see it. I screamed and leaped across the room and snatched the toy away, telling him off. Cathryn seemed a little disgruntled by being nearly suffocated by her brother but James was screaming in distress at having done something wrong.

We were such proud parents. By the time Cathryn was five months old she was becoming quite a little character. She loved her big brother and she would sit and cuddle him and giggle with him. I knew I had done the right thing for James as he learned to love and interact with his sister.

Maternal Instinct

It was May 2003 and Cathryn was nearly six months old. I had intended to stop breast feeding her at that age and was starting to consider how to wean her. There was a stomach bug going around the village children at the time, so when she started vomiting I wasn't overly concerned at first. Yet when she hadn't kept any milk down for a day and didn't seem herself at all, I took her to the GP.

By this time, she was throwing up brown liquid which I thought must be bile as she had no more food to bring up. I had her wrapped in a towel which had some of this 'bile' on it which she had thrown up on the journey to the surgery. Unfortunately, we got to see a locum who completely dismissed my concerns as basically an overwrought new mother. If he had bothered to look at my records he would have seen that I was not a constant feature at the surgery. He didn't have any advice for me. I asked him for something to help hydrate her but he was reluctant to give me anything. I also asked what to do if she didn't soon stop throwing up. He told me to come back if she went floppy.

What ensued was three days of hell, where I tried to get my baby, who was obviously in some pain as she cried and kept arching her back, to feed and keep something down. I was contacted by the health visitor though she didn't visit, she did speak to me on the 'phone a few times. I remember sitting on the stairs holding Cathryn in my arms whilst describing how I'd been trying to feed her and how she threw up every time. I was exhausted. I hadn't slept for days.

In the end, I rang NHS Direct, the non-emergency line as I was so concerned about Cathryn. She hadn't had a wet

105

nappy for three days. This was significant. The nurse I spoke to insisted I take her immediately take her to the nearest A and E. I stupidly asked if that would be our local town and they said if it was my nearest hospital, then yes. We took our limp baby to the run down, understaffed emergency centre, who told us she was a bit dehydrated but they didn't deal with children there. They didn't seem too concerned but arranged for us to be admitted to emergency at Newcastle General. This was a thirty-minute drive away. I was terrified with all this delay I was going to lose my baby. When we got to Newcastle, the female paediatrician took one look at Cathryn in my arms and insisted that the staff put Cathryn on a drip straight away.

To our relief, Cathryn started to revive on the ward and soon after they took her off to x-ray to find out what was causing her problem. It turned out not to be a stomach bug at all but an intussusception where her bowel was twisted and was allowing nothing through. She had been starving. We started to think that this would be the end of our nightmare. The medical team at the General were not specialist enough to deal with her problem so we were transferred to the larger hospital nearby.

I travelled in the ambulance holding Cathryn but for some unknown reason, she was not transferred with her drip and when she got to the Royal Victoria Infirmary, she deteriorated again, very quickly. She had a team of paediatricians working on her and I was standing anxiously by, not knowing what to do. One of the doctors remarked how cold she was and asked me if she had some socks. I went off to find some little pink socks but they never got used. In hindsight, they possibly just wanted me out of the room.

The team of doctors could not get a drip into her tiny veins and my baby went into shock. It was possibly the worst moment of my life when I heard them call the crash team to my daughter. I just sat in a corner in shock myself while the team worked on her.

David in the meantime had parked the car and gone shopping. He had thought everything was fine. I was left alone sitting on a hospital chair witnessing all this in a haze. By the time he came back I don't think it had dawned on him what was happening. The consultant took us to a side room and gently explained what was happening. He told us she needed an operation immediately. I signed the papers without any hesitation though I didn't think I would ever see my baby again.

David was trying to encourage me to eat but my whole body had shut down. How could he expect me to eat at a time like this? I don't know if he had any concept of how bad I felt. For reassurance, he managed to get hold of his sister on his mobile and told her what was going on. I think he came off the 'phone paler as she was honest with him about the seriousness of the situation.

They prepared Cathryn for surgery and wheeled her passed us on the trolley. She looked so tiny. The consultant was wonderful and I think he knew exactly what I was going through. He asked me if I wanted to kiss her goodbye before she went in. Normally I would pooh-pooh such a sentiment but I really did want to. I felt it was the last time I would see her alive.

We were put in a family room and a young doctor came to talk to us. He wanted to know exactly what had happened in the last few days. Even though he was pleasant, I felt I was being judged as a bad mother. I wished I hadn't listened to the GP and had acted sooner.

I was convinced that even if Cathryn survived she would be taken away from us for neglect. I can't remember how long we waited but it felt like forever. Eventually, the consultant came to us and told us she was fine. They had cut out the knotted piece of bowel causing the obstruction, taken out her appendix 'just in case' and amazingly he said they had found a very rare condition called Meckel's Diverticulum, which they had also removed. If she had not been operated on for the intussusception, she would probably have died when the Meckel's Diverticulum had turned septic later. Apparently, it was a difficult condition to diagnose in time.

We crept in to see her shortly afterwards but she was still under the effects of the anaesthetics. There was a huge amount of relief but I think I was just numb with the strain and exhaustion. It's just a blur.

We decided not to stay the night as we were utterly exhausted after days of no sleep. There were no facilities immediately available and there wasn't anything I could do for her. I felt if I didn't get some sleep I might have another panic attack. We got home that night and slept like the dead. James was still with his grandma, so we got up early and went straight back to the children's ward. The nurses were smiling when we arrived and they pointed to where Cathryn was sitting up waving a rattle, smiling and laughing. We couldn't believe our eyes. Our gorgeous happy baby had been restored to us.

I stayed in hospital with Cathryn for a few more days until her bowels started working again. My mum and dad popped in to see us several times, terribly worried about their first granddaughter. My mum brought a beautiful, fluffy, white seal for Cathryn which was bigger than she was.

After a couple of days, the doctors said I could introduce a little food for Cathryn to try. I gave her a tiny bit of porridge. She wolfed it down and demanded more. I wasn't sure if I should but she was so hungry, so I did. Shortly after I was holding her when she threw up an enormous amount of green vomit all over me. I was covered and didn't have a change of clothes.

Mum stayed with me while I sent David to the shops. There was a Marks and Spencer's just a few minutes' walk away. He was gone for nearly two hours. I was still wearing the vomit covered top when he got back. He was breathing heavily, quite agitated and angry and for some reason he had several bags with him. He angrily ranted at me for not being able to find any clothes shops in town.

He had eventually gone to an outdoor shop and found me several t shirts and he didn't know which one I would like. His overreaction made me feel guilty and stressed, as if it was all my fault. It hadn't occurred to me to have to tell him where Marks and Spencer's was. It was literally just down the street from the hospital and had been there for years. He must have known. Yet in his distress he had walked in completely the opposite direction.

After a week, it was a relief to get home and get our life back on track. My friends in the village had all been fantastic and rallied around. Prayers had been said in church for Cathryn people had left baskets of flowers on our doorstep. We had offers of help from friends and neighbours who were all concerned. I was so glad we had moved to this friendly and beautiful part of Northumberland.

The locum who had dismissed my fears was apparently severely reprimanded and we were told that our local health centre would never be using his services again. I didn't want to take it any further. I just hoped he had learned his lesson.

Independence

In July, James found out he was leaving pre-school and going to Big School. Big School was a hundred yards down the road and he had enjoyed his visit there with his eight other classmates. On his last day at pre-school the staff threw a big party. We said goodbye to all his lovely teachers and started walking home for the start of the six-week summer holidays. When we got to the path that leads down to the Packhorse Bridge, our usual way home, James tugged on my hand.

"What's the matter?" I asked him.

"Big School's not that way," he told me firmly. "It's this way," and he pointed beyond the church towards the First School.

"But it's Going Home Time." I reminded him. He looked confused and started to cry and was trying to drag me down the road towards the school.

He reminded me adamantly that the preschool leader had told them that they were going to Big School *now*. I started to giggle as I realised that he had taken her literally. He thought he was going directly from preschool to start at Big School that day.

I crouched down and explained to him that he would be going to Big School soon but first he would be having a six-week break and so would his friends. He eventually accepted this and skipped happily down the hill. We stopped off at the playpark on the way home so he could run around with his friends in the sun.

Independence

James turned four at the end of August, a week before he started at the village school. He was very much looking forward to going as he was ready to learn. He had already demanded to be taught basic words, much to his reception teacher's annoyance. He spent most of the day playing with the train set on the floor with his best friend. I was not one of the tearful parents.

Around this time, I started taking driving lessons again. I was keen for more independence and hated having to travel around by bus, especially with two young children. The local buses hardly ever arrived on time and twice I had been refused entry onto the bus because they didn't have room for a pushchair.

When I had first moved in with David he had soon suggested that I learned to drive. I had a few lessons before I went to London and even took my test but I was so nervous I mucked it up. When I returned, I was so busy working, getting married and then getting pregnant, the subject didn't come up for ages. After that we were a bit skint. When I was pregnant with Cathryn though I decided to have another go.

I was nine months pregnant when I took my test at the local centre and was dreadfully nervous. Despite this I had a perfect test until I was asked to turn back into the side road towards the test centre. I had to stop for oncoming traffic and was aware I was holding traffic up behind me. I felt very pressured and when I saw a gap in the traffic, I went for it. Unfortunately, I had forgotten to go into first gear and stalled the car. I panicked and turned the ignition on and off so many times, I didn't know where I was. When I finally got going, my driving instructor said he had never seen anyone drive back in so fast. I had failed again!

I was so mad with myself. I decided to give up for the duration. David was very sympathetic. He knew I was a good driver and encouraged me to drive him around and was and patient with me in the beginning.

Setting off from home one Saturday morning with the kids in the back, I noticed David was in completely the wrong gear. I helpfully pointed this out. He turned to me and snarled,

"When you've learned to drive, then you can tell me what to do!"

I was absolutely devastated by what he said. He knew how sensitive I was about this subject and he might as well have slapped me in the face. I didn't let him know how much he hurt me though.

On 13th November 2003, I took my driving test again and to my absolute joy, this time I passed! I hadn't told a soul other than David. Linda came to look after Cathryn but I just told her I had a driving lesson. Without the added pressure of people's expectations, I amazed myself by passing. I had to get the examiner to repeat himself, I was so stunned. I couldn't wait to tell David. He was genuinely pleased for me and didn't waste time getting me insured on to our family car.

The first time I went out by myself I was terribly nervous. I stalled the car five times before even leaving our street. Once I managed to get onto the main road I was okay and decided to go for a gentle drive up the A68. I had never done this before, even accompanied and it turned out to be a huge mistake. In my naivety, I hadn't realised how aggressively everybody drove up that road. They kept hassling and over taking me and I found it impossible to turn off for miles. I had to pull over to calm myself down. I drove home through the countryside, past Slaley Hall and eventually found my way home. I had been over an hour and David was quite agitated by the time I got back. I think he had envisioned all kinds of disasters happening in that time.

David had recently had the 'snip' as we knew we didn't want any more children. A boy and a girl was just perfect for us and, I knew I wouldn't be able to cope with three. I would need much more help from David if we did and I was realistic about whether I would get that. When we spoke to the GP about it he had to make sure we knew what we were doing. He pointed out that if one of our children died we wouldn't be able to have any more. I was horrified at what he said. Children are not like puppies. You can't just replace them when you lose one. That thought was reinforced that day as I was waiting for Cathryn to come out of surgery. The love I had for my daughter was so strong and even at six months of age she was a real character. I knew in my heart if we lost her that I wouldn't want to replace her.

David had pretty much volunteered to go through with it. He said that it was his turn as I had been the one to go through pregnancy and birth with the kids. I appreciated his willingness to do this for us very much. Continuing to take the pill was just not an option for me.

So, I found myself one week after having passed my test, driving to the hospital with David's sperm sample under my armpit. I located an empty space in the busy car-park and smiling to myself, managed to find the correct room in the hospital to hand it in. Getting back into the car though, I had a dreadful time manoeuvring out of the parking space. I was terrified I was going to scratch the car and just couldn't figure out how to reverse out safely. I'd always assumed it was such a simple manoeuvre!

To compound matters, a car parked up alongside me, indicating they would use my space the moment I left. Additional pressure! I put my head in my hands for a moment before trying to manoeuvre again. After another failed attempt the driver got out of her car and asked if I needed any help. I found myself nearly in tears, confessing that I'd just passed my test and they should never have passed me. She was very sympathetic but realised I just needed to be allowed to work it out myself.

Eventually, I did get out without any damage to any car and drove home quite shaken. I realised that getting through the test had been easy compared to being let loose on the roads by myself.

As an early Christmas present, David bought me a new pre-registered Renault Clio. I didn't get to choose the colour or anything about it, but it was new and it was cheap. I got my confidence driving around in that. Is it wrong to say that passing my driving test and getting my first car were more exciting than getting married? It made much more of a difference to my life than gaining a joint bank account ever could.

Denial

In 2004, my mum's cancer returned with a vengeance. She kept it quiet and though I knew it was back, I didn't realise how bad it was. I think I assumed that she had survived it before and would do so again. I was too caught up with my own family problems to give it enough thought or maybe I was just in denial.

David was very unhappy at work and I had been trying to get him to look for a new job for at least a year but he was always too busy to do so. The atmosphere at the company had changed from when he had first started working there. He was no longer paid overtime but on a flat rate which was far less than we were used to because of the ridiculous hours David had always worked. This didn't stop David from working those same hours however. There was talk of redundancy and David was terrified he would be let go as he was one of the more highly-paid members of staff. It was very difficult to talk to him about anything, especially money as we were finding it hard to cope on reduced amounts already.

I secretly wished that he would be made redundant as then he didn't have any choice other than to find a new job. My wish came true but David was devastated. Though I was quietly pleased, I knew we were getting a comfortable pay off so wouldn't be left penniless. I was horrified and angry at the way David had been treated. He had had a meeting with the directors, who had assessed him on his strengths and weaknesses. David had scored highly in most areas of his work as you would expect. The area that had apparently let him down, was 'Taking leave without notice'. The only time that David had done this was when Cathryn had been

116

dying in hospital. Everyone in the company knew exactly what had been going on and had sent their best wishes to us via several cards and bouquets of flowers. It was obviously a complete ambush. We hadn't realised we had had to book our child's near-death experience in with the director's first, especially when David consistently went above and beyond for them at every turn.

David went to the Job Centre for the first time in his life. I didn't know what to expect when he came back from his interview but I think he had bombarded them with information rather than the other way around. He gained £50 in entitlement for that week. He needn't have worried though. As soon as certain companies heard that David was available, they were ringing him up to offer him a job. He ended up working for a government funded research unit within a week, on a better salary than he had been on the week before.

Also, that week, David was offered his old job under a new title, at a vastly-reduced rate. I don't know if this was legal but it certainly wasn't ethical. Thankfully, we didn't have to consider it for a second, and they were told in no uncertain terms what to do with their job offer.

Alone

We both absolutely adored the kids but showed it in very different ways. David would do practical jobs like construct toys or fix DVD players, whilst I did the hands-on caring and disciplining. I didn't ask for it to be left to me but the times he interfered were often devastating for both me and the kids. He would overreact terribly if the kids stepped out of line at all, something they rarely did.

When James was tiny, we stopped eating out as David couldn't' bear the embarrassment of other diners thinking we were bad parents with a crying baby. As James got older, he was a very well-behaved child and we were happy to take him to family restaurants. His favourite was TGI Fridays and he insisted on having the same meal every time we went.

His younger sister was now about two and starting to enjoy proper food. She was a very happy child, smiley and chatty and excitable at times like any other toddler. We had taken them both to our local TGI Friday's restaurant a few times before and not had a problem. On this occasion, Cathryn was being a bit silly and messing about in her highchair. James was reacting to his sister and I had to try and quieten them down as David was getting very agitated.

We ordered our food but Cathryn was still a little excitable. David was getting cross and saying that everyone was looking at us and muttering that we were bad parents. I looked worriedly around to see if we were bothering other people. It was already a noisy restaurant, busy with other chatting families with young children, loud music and loud staff. I didn't think we were causing a problem. I expect I voiced this. Suddenly, he got up and just walked out, leaving me alone with the children. I didn't know if he had just gone to get some fresh air or driven off. I didn't know what to do as our food hadn't even arrived yet and I had two hungry, expectant children. I couldn't exactly run out after him, leaving two young children behind in the restaurant. I didn't know if he expected me to or not. I hoped he would come back in in a few minutes. He didn't.

It wasn't easy to stay calm and pretend that all was fine. I told the questioning staff he was on a business call. Thankfully, we had ordered something to share but I could barely bring myself to eat anything. At least I had my purse with me. As quickly as I could, I paid and left with the kids. Still pretending everything was fine. I hoped to find him waiting outside.

He was sitting in the car with a foul look on his face. I was obviously in the wrong. Was I meant to walk out of the restaurant leaving the kids or not paying to see if he was okay?

We didn't speak all the way home.

Detached

I think David and I were getting along much better due to increased confidence and our sudden reduction of money worries. We started to address the other problem in our lives which was the size of our house and the proximity of our neighbours. We had hardly done anything to it. We saw a house in the village that was larger and detached and put an offer in on it. The pompous estate agent who had encouraged us to view the house and put ours on the market, then informed us that we had been gazumped but as if he had had nothing to do with it. We decided to move anyway and put our pretty Edwardian villa on the market, with a different agent.

I found a big old farm house which we decided to rent whilst we were looking. It was half a mile up a bumpy gravel track, off the main road, four miles outside of the village. The 1920's farm house had large square rooms, four bedrooms and a huge garden. The views were to die for and I fell in love with it.

The letting agent informed me it wasn't as simple as I thought to rent the place. This was a farm house on a country estate and the owners liked to have good quality, long-term tenants. I had to fill in a long application form and with advice from my friends, I wrote a letter to the estate owners informing them what good tenants we would be. We had to wait a couple of weeks for a decision.

In the meantime, my mother's health deteriorated rapidly. She was spending most of her time in bed and was barely able to get to the loo in time. She could hardly make it up and down the stairs. Dad didn't seem that worried about her failing condition. Mum was very calm and matter of fact about her condition and hardly mentioned it. This left me confused. I didn't know how worried I should be.

The week before, I had driven her to the nearest hospital as she was complaining about her arm not feeling right. She thought she had broken it but didn't know how. On examination, it turned out the bone in her forearm had snapped due to the cancer. I was horrified when I realised it was in her bones. She was taken into hospital and operated on to insert a rod into her arm. I picked her up on the Friday morning. She seemed in good spirits. Mum had spent most of her time on the ward helping the nurses and chatting to the other patients who tended to be a lot older than her.

On the Sunday, David and I took the kids to the beach and popped in to see mum and dad as we were passing. Dad said mum wasn't feeling very well, that she was in a lot of pain and using breathing techniques to help with the pain. He said this quite proudly. I thought this was very odd. I was extremely concerned that her morphine tablets weren't helping anymore. I went into her bedroom to see her. She looked terrible. I had James with me and she told me to take him away. I was really worried about her but my dad seemed to think everything was fine.

The following morning, as I dropped James off at school my dad rang and asked me to come. Again, he didn't sound too bothered, but I had a terrible feeling about it. I took Cathryn to David's mother on the way over to Whitley Bay.

It took me about forty minutes to get there. As I walked in the back door, a Macmillan nurse walked in through the front. My dad had said there was already one there so I was concerned to see there were two. My mum was lying in bed looking terribly pale but conscious. I sat down on the edge of the bed as I had often done before but she winced in pain.

I found space on the chair next to her instead. She asked me where James was. I said he was at school and that he was having his first recorder lesson that day. She gave a little laugh. I could tell she was in a lot of pain but I didn't know what else to do other than talk a little. The nurses were hovering around and making sure she was as comfortable as possible. It was slowly dawning on me that this was not good.

My dad came into the room and said he was going to the shop to get something. As he left, my mum asked him to get her some 'bendy straws'. She had been having difficulty drinking out of a cup whilst in bed. My dad cheerfully went off to the shop at the end of the street. In the meantime, my mum got worse. I held her hand as she moaned and groaned. By the time he came back she had gone very quiet. Her hand was freezing. I knew then she was going to die. The nurses had hardly said anything. I think they must have thought I was expecting this. Mum's breathing became quite erratic and for the first time in my life I heard and identified the death rattle.

My dad wandered back into the room. He had no clue what was going on. I told him he needed to come and hold mum's hand.

"Why?" he asked. I couldn't bring myself to say why, but I insisted that he do it.

He agreed and sat on the chair I had just vacated and held her hand. Seconds later she died. It took a long moment for it to dawn on my dad what had just happened. She just lay there still and peaceful. He looked at her.

"Jenny? Jenny?" he kept repeating. I stood behind him and put my hand on his shoulder.

"Dad, she's gone." I gently told him.

He sat at the side of her bed in shock. He'd genuinely had no idea that this would happen. I realise now my mum had protected us all and not let on quite how ill she was. She had made light of every stage of her deterioration. I understand now why she did it. My dad couldn't handle the information but I wish she'd been more honest with me. On the other hand, maybe she couldn't face up to it either.

Apparently, she had told my dad that morning that she was going to die and to tell the kids she loved them. He had told her not to be so silly.

The first person I rang was David. Thankfully, he was working nearby in Blyth. I cried down the 'phone to him. He dropped everything and came straight away. He was wonderful, giving me a huge hug when he walked into my parent's hallway. He was very supportive and dashed around doing lots of things I couldn't do. The next person I rang was my brother Nicholas who was also at work. I had no idea what his work number was, so had to dial Directory Enquiries. It was a nightmare getting through the tele'phone maze at pharmaceutical company but eventually I got hold of him. By this time, I just burst out,

"Nick, Mum's died!"

He made me explain a bit more before he also dropped everything and came straight over. He went up to mum's room where dad was still sitting with her body.

The worst thing was getting hold of my little sister. Rhiannon was seventeen and studying at High School. It was May and she was about to take her A-levels. I was so glad of David's support as he rang the school and explained what was going on. He asked the staff only to tell her to meet us outside the school. We drove up and I jumped out of the car. I wanted to hold it together for her and tell her as gently as possible but I couldn't. As I ran up to Rhiannon waiting by the school wall I again burst into tears and cried,

"It's mum, she's dead!"

The look on my sister's face was unfathomable, and she didn't say anything. I sat in the back of the car with her and cuddled her on the way home.

She didn't want to go in to mum's room but reluctantly agreed. To be honest it wasn't a nice sight but I think she needed to see her. She didn't stay long.

David went out to the local supermarket to get some food. Everyone sat in the living room talking and chomping comfort food of pizza and doughnuts. Except me. I couldn't eat. I sat there astounded that people could eat at a time like that.

I had rung David's mum and told her what had happened. Linda had burst into tears and told me that she would be my mum from now on. I knew she meant well but I wasn't ready to hear it.

After a bit, I think David must have gone back to work as he had left something at a crucial point. I didn't mind as he had been a great help and I had calmed down and had my family around me. I don't remember who rang our eldest sibling, Rhys to tell him. It was probably Nick.

During this lull, the doorbell of my parents' house rang loudly. I answered the door. It was my sister's friends Emma and Alfie from school. I think they must have come to see if she was okay. Rhiannon came to the door and told them she was fine and when they asked if she wanted to come out she told them that she didn't'. She didn't tell them what had happened and she didn't let them in.

It was about two o'clock in the afternoon and I needed to get back to pick James up. It felt wrong to leave at such a time but everything else had been dealt with for now and James would be expecting me. I drove off down Marine Avenue as if nothing had happened.

On the way, I passed Emma and Alfie. I pulled the car up and ran across the busy road to speak to them. I realised that my sister hadn't been able to explain what had been going on. I quickly explained to them what had happened. Their jaws dropped, they hadn't even known our mum was ill. Rhiannon hadn't told them anything.

I must have picked Cathryn up from Linda's on the way back, but I don't remember. I just remember standing in the school yard at quarter past three, waiting for James's Reception Class to come out, desperately hoping that no one would speak to me or I would burst into tears, there and then.

I got home to find an answer-machine message from the letting agent saying that we had been chosen from several applicants to live in Fairley May Farm House. It was the most anti-climactic moment of my life. The day before I had been on tenterhooks about this decision and now I just felt numb.

My close friend Charlotte, Cathryn's godmother offered to come to the funeral with me which was so thoughtful of her. I thanked her and turned her down as she wouldn't have known anyone but I really appreciated the offer. Looking back now, I really value not just my childhood friends, but my more recently acquired village friends who were sympathetic and supportive.

As the elder daughter, a lot of the onus was on me. I needed to be there for my sister as well as my dad. He was in a complete state of shock. I must have driven over to see him nearly every day before the funeral. He just wanted to talk. He told me that he had woken up that morning with tears pouring down his face. I was desperately sad for him. They had been married for thirty-eight years and had rarely been apart. They bickered and complained about each other all the time but I knew they loved each other.

In a way though, I was more worried about Rhiannon. I remembered back to Mother's Day earlier that year, when mum had been in tears. She had predicted what would happen. She and Rhiannon had not been getting on. Rhiannon was being a typical teenager and not communicating with either mum or dad. Yet, I think at the same time she was scared. She knew mum wasn't well and didn't know how to deal with her illness. Instead of talking to my mum about her fears, she stayed out of her way. Mum had basically said that she wished Rhiannon would talk to her. Mum knew what it was like to lose a parent so young, as her beloved father had died suddenly when she was eighteen. I must have been in denial myself at the time because I thought this was a hypothetical conversation; not a prophecy.

Rhiannon had not seen mum on the day she died. She had not been in to see her to say goodbye before she went to school. I don't know how a teenager deals with grief, especially not when it is tinged with guilt which I suspect it was. I spent quite a lot of time with her. We went shopping and surprisingly had a nice day, choosing her funeral outfit. We did talk – a bit.

The day of my mother's funeral, 17th May 2004, was both terrible and wonderful. The church of St Paul's in Whitley Bay was packed. There were so many family and friends that turned up from Cardiff and around the country, congregants from the church and a coach load of people from my mum's work. We had a lot of people come back to the house and it was lovely to see and talk to friends and family we hadn't seen in ages. My dad coped remarkably well. He was being looked after by some good friends. David was an absolute star that day. He was dashing about sorting out food and drink, introducing people and sorting out any problems our guests had. If something was needed, he got it. If someone needed driving somewhere he took them. He made himself very useful. At times like that people often remark on how helpful and fantastic he is. He will always solve other people's problems.

The following day, a number of visiting friends and family filled our little house. I had the keys to the farmhouse and asked them if they would like to visit. A convoy of cars followed David and me up the hill and along the, pot-holed farm track. There was quite a cloud of dust that could be seen from a distance with all the cars joggling over the potholes. There was more than enough room in the car park for everyone. It was good to take our minds off mum for a moment as we showed everyone around our new, empty home. I remember sitting on the windowsill at the top of the stairs with my dad surveying the fields and hills spread out before us. He commented that my mum would have loved this. I knew he was right.

For weeks after the funeral I would find myself in floods of tears about mum. For once, David was supportive and never complained about my excess emotion. Maybe this was because he knew it wasn't aimed at him. He too missed my mum and perhaps in some way I was expressing grief for both of us.

Gaining some Space

In the middle of June, the sale of our house was completed and we moved in to the farmhouse. It was a bright sunny day and the Northumbrian countryside views were stunning. The removal men were having difficulty carrying all our furniture into the house as it was so windy outside but there was more than enough space for everything.

Once the removal men had gone, David and I found a space on the sofa and relaxed for the first time in months. We realised that we and the children could make as much noise as we wanted and no one would hear us. The kids had their own playroom filled with toys, where they could make as much mess as they wanted. All I had to do was shut the door on it. It took me a few weeks to stop feeling tense when the kids shouted and screamed about something but I did start to relax. I hadn't known how tense we had been by living in the house with paper-thin walls.

I know for some people that living in the middle of a field, miles from anywhere is hell but for us it was bliss. Okay, we had to get in the car if we wanted to go anywhere but we had a spacious house with half-an-acre of garden for our kids to run around in. We were only a few minutes' drive away from the village and school itself and some of my closest friends happened to live nearby.

Parenting

By this time, Cathryn was a lively eighteen-month-old. She was such a happy child. Everyone who came in to contact with her adored her. Who could resist those big blue eyes and the sweet, happy smile. She, in turn, adored her big brother and wanted to be like him. She was also obsessed with *Thomas the Tank Engine and Friends*, though she preferred cheeky Percy, as her favourite colour was green. By this age, she had already toilet-trained herself as she wanted to wear *Thomas the Tank Engine* pants like her big brother. I have pictures of her trip-trapping around the wooden floor of the play room in her Thomas pyjamas and high-heeled, pink *Barbie* slippers.

James was doing well in school apart from having toileting problems. He didn't have many accidents in school though he did occasionally come out in the playground with the carrier bag of shame. The main problem I had with him was trying to get him to do a poo on the toilet. He just wouldn't. I had spoken to the Health Visitor about it many times and we had tried everything from bribery to books. Every time he needed the toilet we would sit and read *Where Poo Goes*. He loved that book but he still wouldn't go. I ended up having a long chat with the school nurse about it.

I didn't discuss parenting problems with David. I would talk to my friends about it and we would share advice. I hardly ever saw David as he was working long hours again. I think he just let me make all the parenting decisions. Most of the time I was happy with that because at least there was consistency there, but sometimes I needed to discuss problems with him and he just didn't want to talk about them or he would get flustered and cross. In the end, it was better to say nothing. I would have long chats with my friends instead.

In the evenings, we would sit together and watch some TV. One of David's favourite programmes was Supernanny. He would sit there and watch and judge other parents with badly behaved children go through therapy and get advice from experts. He was proud that we didn't have any of these problems. We didn't have those behavioural problems because I provided safe, secure and consistent parenting to both our children. The way he spoke was so hypocritical. You would think he was Superdad!

Cathryn started pre-school at the age of two and a half and I started to have a little time to myself. I began going to the gym on the mornings I dropped her off. I enjoyed a little bit of 'me' time, but by lunchtime I was always desperate to pick her up again. She was the source of sunshine in my life, and still is.

A local poet who I knew from church, approached me and offered me a job to type up his poetry, translations, and help with a book he was writing. The pay wasn't great but it was paid work for a change. I was forever busy doing voluntary work for village organisations which took up far too much of my time and for which I rarely got any thanks. I enjoyed doing William's work and it gave me a little self-esteem and some extra cash in my pocket.

William was an academic who worked in London during the week and came back to the family home at the weekend. Once I had typed up his work I would pop along to his beautiful Georgian terraced-house and we would sit and drink green tea, which is quite an acquired taste. We didn't talk much about his work but what was going on in the world. Sometimes Cathryn would come and he would try and entertain her with activities like cleaning out his fish tank. One day he decided we needed to have a sing-song. The piano was down in his basement and he started playing and encouraging me to join in. I found myself singing,

"I love to go a wandering along the mountain track, and as I go I love to sing with my back-pack on my back. Fal-de-ree, fal-de-raa!"

Cathryn loved it.

Believing my Eyes

The summer holidays were coming to an end and the children and I had spent their last free afternoon in the local park with a group of friends. On the way home, I had James sitting in the front of the car on his booster seat and Cathryn had fallen asleep in the back. As we rounded the last bend on the track up to our house, I spotted something large and black on the road up ahead. At first when I squinted, I thought it was just a large crow, but as we came up the rise I saw it was a large black animal. I commented on this to James that it must be the neighbour's large but friendly Staffordshire terrier.

As the car got nearer, we realised it was nothing of the sort. There in the middle of the track, on a blazing August afternoon, was a large black panther sunbathing. I stopped the car in astonishment several yards away. The cat casually glanced at us and then got up and leaped over the five-foot-high, dry stone wall on the far side of the track. It went in one bound with its tail right out behind it. I got out of the car to see where it had gone but it was nowhere to be seen.

It was a surreal moment but I didn't for one second doubt what we had seen. I had read in the *Hexham Courant*, our weekly local newspaper just the week before that there had been a sighting of this very cat. In fact, the sighting had been in the local woods no more than a mile away from our

131

house. Of course, when we had first read it, we had scoffed about the existence of a black panther living nearby. Now I knew for certain it was true. I told James all about this as we travelled the rest of the way home in the car. I said I'd read about it in the paper. He got quite excited in the way that five year olds do and insisted that we should tell the paper. I wasn't sure about that, as I wasn't comfortable with attention seeking. When we got in though, I immediately did a search on the internet about wild cats in the UK. It turned out that in the 1970's, a licensing law was brought in for people who owned wild cats. This unpopular law made it very expensive for the owners but instead of them responsibly finding new homes for these cats in zoos etc., many were just released to fend for themselves. It was quite remarkable, but made sense of what we had just witnessed.

I sent a brief email to the local Courant, saying that I had just seen the cat on my drive, just to keep James happy. I thought if they were at all interested they would contact me for more details. They didn't contact me, so apart from telling David our strange story I forgot all about it. The nice thing about having an Asperger husband is that he doesn't doubt you when you tell him things like that.

The following Friday, when I got to the school playground I was getting a few odd looks from people. Charlotte told me I was on the front of the Courant. Completely clueless I gasped,

"Why? What have I done?"

She had the paper in her hand and showed me. There, on the front page was my email, converted verbatim into a small column about seeing the black cat.

I was quite amused, though couldn't understand why they hadn't followed it up and contacted me to check any details. However, after a few weeks of people constantly questioning me about whether I had actually seen it,

"Yes,"

whether perhaps maybe it had been a Labrador,

"No,"

or an ordinary cat seen at a distance,

"No, it was really quite close and was an actual panther not a house cat,"

I was bored to tears and somewhat annoyed that people would doubt me. I wish I had not given in to James's pleas for publicity.

There was another sighting mentioned in the paper in 2013 and I would love to get in touch with the man, a local plumber just to discuss it with him. We should probably set up a support group for spotters of the black cat.

It was shortly after my brief, local fame, that I spotted an advert in the *Hexham Courant* for village correspondents. Each week, active villages in the Tyne Valley, would employ a local resident to report events that had happened, or were about to happen. Without telling anyone, I contacted the Editor and was surprised to get an interview. I was very nervous as this was my first interview for ages and this was a job that I was keen to get. Colin was very friendly and chatty. He said he had researched my background by using Google and the papers' archives.

I groaned as I realised what he was going to say next. The Black Cat.

We had a laugh about it but thankfully moved on to discuss my education and publishing background. When the editor asked me what strengths I could bring to the article I explained that I was involved in many of the things that were going on in the village. My husband was chair of the parish council; I was secretary of the village halls trust; I was a school governor; ran the toddler group; was an active pre-school committee member; secretary of the PTA and a long-standing member of the Choral Society.

He was impressed with my credentials and contacts and made noises about me maybe becoming a member of the editorial team in the future.

I was even more surprised when he offered me the job and that there was some money involved too. I had assumed that it was a voluntary position. I was on a high as I left his offices in Hexham and went to pick my children up from their schools, until one of the mum's commenting with surprise on my smartness picked a large, dusty cobweb off the back of my suit jacket. I hoped Colin hadn't noticed, but I suspect he had.

I agonised over my first little article, though I had plenty to say. I must have revised the wording many times before I was satisfied. Then I made the mistake of showing it to David before I emailed my 500 words in. I had mentioned something to do with the Parish Council, of which he had recently become Chairman and he was extremely upset about it and insisted I take it out. There was nothing wrong with what I had written and I was angry that he was trying to take over my new writing career. I decided not to ask his opinion after that.

I received a positive response from people in the village and even increased sales of the paper locally. They relished having our village finally on the map and many of them thought my articles were amusing. I was occasionally stopped in the street by complete strangers who must have worked out who I was, and complimented on my work. It was good for my self-esteem and I felt I was starting to use my brain after so long time of just being a mum.

Theory of Mind

We had got ourselves into a financial fix as David had again agreed to a massive pay decrease. We were living beyond our means and starting to use up our savings. Again, he wouldn't listen to me when I said he needed to get a new job where he would be appreciated and paid what he was worth. His self-esteem at the time must have been very low. Eventually, he agreed and signed up with a few employment agencies. Quickly, he had some interviews and was offered contracting work with in Aberdeen. This meant he either worked from home or was commuting to Aberdeen for a few days each week.

David's self-esteem rose quickly as he settled in and found that he got on very well with his new boss. Alan was also from the north-east and though at first, he had reportedly found David a little 'cold', once David became more relaxed and Alan began to see his true worth, they became and still are, very good friends. In a way, Alan was a godsend for us as he was very quick to praise David for his work and David thrived on his praise. Not only was he being paid well but he was being appreciated and that made our home life so much happier.

It took both of us a little while to get used to David becoming a self-employed contractor who mostly worked from home. He was used to his twice-daily commute and I was used to organising my own time and my life revolving around the kids. David commandeered the study full-time while I tried to carry on as normal. I made sure he was fed and watered if I was at home, but I didn't hang around specially to make him coffee. He would often close the door on us if he had an important 'phone call, so I decided it was best to pretend he wasn't there for most of the day.

I think whilse David had been office-based, that he had no concept of mine or the children's' routines and habits during a typical week. From the moment he left the house, to the moment he returned in the evening, he barely gave us a thought. I never got a 'phone call and he never answered my texts. I only rang him on the office 'phone if it was an emergency. This was something I had grown used to over the years. We didn't need to live in each other's pockets.

So, it was hard for me, when suddenly, David started querying my movements during the day. He seemed upset if I didn't report in to him my movements. I found this quite cloying and annoying at first. Partly it was guilt as I would find myself saying "I'm off to playgroup," or, "I'm off to have coffee with Charlotte," and he would say every time,

"Lucky you!"

During the first week, he was working from home and not in Aberdeen, I had been at a friend's house for coffee. We timed our chat to end five minutes before school finished and we would arrive in the playground as the kids came out into the yard. Walking up the path into the schoolyard I saw David standing awkwardly to the side, away from anyone else. Instantly, my heart beat faster as I thought there must be a serious problem and he had come to find me.

"What's the matter?" I asked. "What are you doing here?" He looked at me slightly annoyed.

"Well I didn't know if you were picking James up or not," he answered indignantly.

137

This was one of those moments when I felt like I was going mad. When had I not picked James up from school? Why would I not do such a thing? Did he think I was such a terrible, forgetful mother? I was flummoxed and quite annoyed. He could tell I was irritated and so he became defensive, as if it was all my fault. Apparently, I hadn't told him my daily itinerary in detail, so he didn't know if he was expected to pick the kids up. He thought he had better come, just in case.

Of course, I now know this was a classic case of an autistic with a deficient theory of mind, with an added dash of paranoia and catastrophization. In his own way, he was just trying to help and show concern.

Change for the Worst

Shortly after I had started writing for the *Hexham Courant* my health deteriorated badly. I had been feeling tired and stressed for some time and I was getting regular headaches. I would find myself going to lie down after lunch and suddenly realise it was three o'clock and time to pick up the kids. I would have to leap in the car and race down the hill to collect them on time.

In March 2006, to my delight, we were snowed in for several days. After we got bored of sledging, the children and I decided to make an animated film using their *Lego* characters. With a lot of input from the kids who were aged three and seven at the time, we made a funny story we called Cow on the Line, using just a web cam and some movie-making software we had been given.

James was fascinated by the way we had to move our characters in such tiny ways for each frame and when we put the short sequences together, how our little character ended up boarding onto a train. As most of the *Lego* belonged to James, we had police cars and ambulances which rather dictated the story. David had observed us having fun and insisted on helping, but in the end, just took over as of course he knew how to 'do it properly'. He spent hours and hours one night working on the sound track alone.

We had nearly finished the animation when one morning I got up and realised I could not see the screen in front of me properly. I thought I had another migraine. Slowly it dawned on me that it was more than a migraine and that my vision was badly affected. I didn't want to admit it to myself but I knew I was probably having the same problem in my good left eye as had happened in my right. I didn't at first

139

admit it to David but eventually I had to. I just couldn't cope. He ended up taking me to the Eye Casualty department in Newcastle, where I was examined at first by concerned nurses and then by intrigued doctors and students. They took many pictures at the back of my eyes to see what was happening and confirmed that I had a bleed. Thankfully, they lasered it, but I still had a lot of high pressure in my eye and fluid around it. I was still in a terrible state. I sat David down one evening and told him that I would probably have to give up driving. This caused a huge problem as we lived miles from anywhere. There was no way we could continue to live in the farmhouse.

The high pressure and fluid on my left eye meant I was on a lot of medication and not only did I have to give up driving I had to resign most of my responsibilities. This was a great relief in some way as I had taken on too much but didn't know how to say No, when asked to do things. Being ill was my way out and I stopped working for William and came off a number of committees. I had to concentrate on myself and the children.

This ended up being the catalyst for change that we needed to move back to the village and buy somewhere. I had been concerned for quite some time that house prices were rising rapidly, but I could not convince David enough to agree to move. I already knew that we could not afford the type of house we could have two years earlier. However, he had stuck his head in the sand as he was too busy working; was comfortable at the farmhouse and hated moving. This had never been our plan. If I ever ventured into the realm of talking about money, he would become extremely angry with me. He could never look at our financial situation without bringing emotion into it. It also depended on whether he had had a good day at work or not.

I felt powerless in this part of our relationship as it had been years since I had brought any significant money in, and though ours was an equal partnership in many ways, David was always the one who would make the decision about large financial acquisitions. However, he was not emotionally equipped to look at our situation dispassionately and see that the longer we stayed in that house, with a rising rent, the less likely we could afford to stay there or get back on the housing ladder.

Within a month of deciding we needed to move, we found a little bungalow that had been empty for some time. We looked around it and saw it had a lot of potential. We couldn't afford the larger houses in the village but knew that with some building work, we could make this little place big enough. As it was a chain-free move, we got the keys within six weeks.

We had to get rid of a lot of furniture and junk which we had acquired over the last two years in the farmhouse. The children had to share a room, so it was quite a squeeze but once we were in it was good to know that we had our own roof over our heads again.

Cathryn started at the village school with her brother that September, so for once I had both children in the same place. She absolutely thrived at the school but James was having difficulties. His teachers were saying he was getting upset regularly and that he wouldn't tell them what the matter was. They said he looked tired and needed more sleep. He was not working very hard and did not want to join in any class activities. I had heard this before but not

141

since he was in preschool. We decided that he was worried about going on to the middle school. Nothing would happen for a few months and then the subject would be raised again. Eventually the headteacher decided to get the educational psychologist involved. By the end of the school year however, they had not been to visit James. I wasn't sure it was necessary anyway.

Renovation

It took us about a year to make any decisions as to what to do with the house. I knew exactly what I wanted to do with our tired little bungalow and what would best suit our family's needs but David didn't have my vision at all. We argued constantly about whether we should do a garage conversion or not. He liked the idea of having his own space to work in, but feared the cost of the additional work. He kept insisting that he could work from the dining room but he would continually shout at the kids to be quiet because he was working in the open-plan environment. It was never going to work. After initially dismissing the need for a garage conversion he later brought up the idea as if it were his own.

David got on well with Nigel as they were both happy talking technical matters, and he was confident in Nigel's abilities to get us through planning. Nigel gave us several good options to extend the house, varying different designs and costs. We could discuss our options more sensibly once the plans were laid out in front of us. If only I had known what a visual thinker David was sooner, we could have resolved many issues without any arguments but he could never understand my verbal descriptions of what I envisaged in my mind's eye.

One of our biggest disagreements, even with the architect's plans, was about the porch I wanted to add to the front of the house. Partly it was for aesthetics, as the bungalow was just a rectangular box from the front with a couple of steps up into the house. It was a typical 1960s utilitarian design. The hallway was very pokey compared to the rest of the house which was surprisingly spacious. Many of our visitors had commented it was like a little 'TARDIS' once you stepped inside. However, with two young children and lots of coats, boots and other paraphernalia to cope with, our hallway was much too small. It was going to cost the least amount of any addition to the house and yet would make the largest practical and visual impact. He grudgingly gave in to me, not because he agreed but because he had got the study and space that he desired.

Having got planning permission, we began the task of finding a builder. This was left up to me. If it wasn't work related, David was never keen to interface with anyone. I was however, more than happy to throw myself in at the deep end and basically, I knew that if I didn't do it, the task would never be done. After a few false starts with unreliable builders, I found Steve, a local builder who came when he said he would and quoted us exactly what we wanted. Our build was to start in November 2007.

It only dawned on us as the build started, how disruptive this was going to be to our lives, and possibly how dangerous it could be with two young children around. The men had only started digging foundation but we knew once they began inside the house, when the weather was bad, it would be impossible to live there.

I had a moment of inspiration and rang some friends in the village who were going away for three months to New Zealand to visit family. I asked if we could rent their house while they were away. They were enthusiastic about this as they had previously had to pay a house-sitter for insurance purposes. We agreed a very decent rent and they said we could move in on Christmas Eve, if we wanted to. At first, David was a bit worried that I had been so cheeky in suggesting this, but when we went to visit Rosemary and

Walter to finalise details, he realised what a good idea it was. I know however, that if I had suggested it to him first he would never have let me approach them. I presented it to him positively as a fait accompli and try as he might he couldn't find anything wrong with the idea. David decided I was genius!

The house we temporarily moved into was up a steep hill on the periphery of the village and was a large four-bedroom detached property. The kids were thrilled as they had separate rooms again and their life was hardly disrupted at all. That was the easy bit.

Steve was a great builder to have. He always turned up on time with his team of cheerful lads and they worked hard. They also kept our neighbour's sweet by cleaning up any mess created at the end of the day. If there was ever a problem with the plans, Steve would communicate with us straight away and he and David would come up with a solution. David seemed to enjoy the 'lads together' mentality, which he was used to from his time spent in large engineering workshops.

What was hard for David was communicating with me. He often didn't tell me what was going on unless I asked. Maybe he thought I wasn't that interested. Just because I didn't understand everything technical, didn't mean I didn't want to know. Also, in my mind's eye, I knew exactly how I wanted the house. David had always been quite happy with my taste in decorating. I would view it as a joint decision as if David didn't like something, I wouldn't insist on it; however, that was rarely a problem as I'm not the type of woman to go in for girly colours and frills. I like unfussy lines and occasional bold statements.

Trying to save money, one Saturday afternoon we went into a little tile showroom in Newcastle. We were looking for ceramic tiles for the kitchen floor. My cabinets that had been chosen were a plain Shaker white and we had gone for black granite worktops. I had found some rectangular tiles that would look great on the floor. However, there was a choice of plain shiny black or a more matte grey. David could not decide at all, and got so angry over our inability to decide, he started talking very patronisingly and very loudly to me in the shop. His volume would increase if there were people nearby, as if he enjoyed an audience. I was both angry and mortified at the patronising way he was treating me. I also couldn't understand why he was getting so stressed over the mere choice between black or grey.

Now it is quite possible, he believed that there was a right and a wrong answer. He was probably cross with me for not giving him the answer when I just wanted to include him in the decision making. There is no right or wrong where personal taste is concerned but that is hard for someone to understand who literally has no concept of style.

In hindsight, I should never have given him the responsibility of even joint decision making. I made the mistake of treating him like a neurotypical man who would probably want to at least be consulted. He on the other hand, when someone asks him his opinion, believes he must give the right answer. His behaviour stemmed from not knowing what the right answer was. I would always start these shopping expeditions with optimism and excitement. I had always wanted to get my teeth into a project and design something to our taste. I would spend hours poring over house and kitchen 'porn' looking at the latest designs and working out how to get something just right, for a reasonable sum. Yet as the amount of money we spent rose, his anxiety rose exponentially. I started to dread these shopping expeditions as he sucked the life and enthusiasm out of me.

Over the months as his anxiety levels grew, the way he treated me became correspondingly worse. Every time the subject of money came up he would get hysterical. He hated talking to me about it. He would imply that I knew nothing and he knew everything. Several times in front of the builders he would start arguments with me. He was rude and aggressive for no reason. I was terribly embarrassed, as I think were they. He couldn't seem to understand what he was doing was wrong. Maybe he likes to sort out disagreements in front of everyone at work, but that was not how he should have been treating his wife. He would be extremely condescending, nasty and rude to me. I was completely bewildered. I did not understand why he was behaving like that.

Meltdown

One Saturday morning, not long before we were due to move back into our renovated bungalow, I was putting the rubbish bins out in the front garden of our rented house. David followed me outside and began ranting at me, accusing me of doing something so utterly unfounded. I completely lost control of my emotions. To this day, I can't remember what he said. I have blocked it out of my memory, but I can still remember how he stunned me with what he accused me of. Something I had done or was doing that he had completely misconstrued. I read recently it is common to have memory black-outs when you are being 'gaslighted' by your partner.

I angrily marched back into the kitchen where he followed me, still ranting. We had a blazing row as for once he had given me no reason to hold back. He harangued me to the point I thought I was going to hit him. Instead, I turned to the side where I saw my favourite and very expensive stainless-steel bin. I took all my frustration out on the poor bin and basically can only describe it as 'kicking the shit' out of it. David stood there and watched me in horror and begged me to stop. He couldn't believe what he was seeing. He rarely saw me lose my temper and he'd never seen me be violent before.

I exerted enough control not to attack him but I couldn't hold in my building anger, frustration and hurt any more.

I told him in no uncertain terms that that was it. I was leaving him. I told the kids to get in the car as we were going. James was seven and Cathryn just turned four. Cathryn was completely unaware of what was going on and happily climbed into her car seat. James however, though a very quiet boy who lives in his own world, at this moment was very astute. He didn't sit down but turned to me and asked,

"Are we leaving Daddy?"

I could see in his eyes he knew what I was going through and he didn't blame me in the slightest. I can't remember what I said, but that comment calmed me down. We were meant to be going to their grandma's, and I didn't really want to turn up there with her asking questions.

I went back in to the house to find David sitting dejected and desolate on the stairs. The look on his face was desperate. I couldn't help feeling a bit sorry for him. I persuaded him to come with us and drop the kids off at his mum's in Newcastle. He eventually agreed to come for appearance's sake but stayed in the car when we arrived. David's mother is used to his moods so she didn't question his behaviour. We automatically drove to Costco as that was our original destination but we didn't get out of the car for an hour. I was still determined to leave him.

The bizarre thing was that he didn't beg me not to. Most women, even if they are desperate to leave a relationship like to be asked to stay, at least once. I think David realised that he had behaved abominably, even if he didn't comprehend exactly what he'd done or why. I told him I was going and that I would take the kids to my dad's in Wales. David was more concerned about how we would survive. He insisted on making sure we would be amply provided for financially. Money was the last thing on my mind, plus I told him I didn't want a penny of his money. I just wanted to get away.

I don't think he realised quite how upset I was until I started to cry. I am normally stoical which is why he can generally cope with me. Up until this point I had just been angry and vocal. Now he didn't know what to do but realised it must be bad if I was crying. This was something he could see but didn't know how to fix.

I was adamant I had had enough and that I was taking the kids away. He seemed to think he deserved it and didn't put up any objections. He didn't ask me not to but bizarrely showed me how much he loved me by supporting me as best he could in what I wanted to do. He thought I was right to go, as he said he was scared of the feelings I had evoked in him. He said he had nearly hit me. We had never been in that position before.

Once I had calmed down, I realised that he still desperately loved me and that I wasn't ready to leave. I didn't know how I felt about him anymore but I didn't hate him. The idea of living with my father also made me think twice. The whole stressful situation of the house renovation had come to a head. It was like pressing the reset button. My feelings started to change as I calmed down and I started to worry about how he would cope without us. Eventually I agreed to stay and we walked into Costco almost as if nothing had happened.

He insisted we get rid of the bin though as he couldn't stand seeing it as a reminder of my temper.

In the April of 2008, we had to move back into our home as the owners were due back from their New Zealand trip. Our house wasn't ready. We did have a kitchen but no floor and we had one working toilet, so we managed but the place was full of men and dust. One morning I hadn't had a chance to get dressed before the workmen arrived. They were still working on our en-suite. While David was talking to them in the hallway I told him I was going to throw some clothes on. Now to most people this piece of information to their husband means, 'I am going into the bedroom to take my pyjamas off and put my clothes on for the day. Don't let anyone in.'

Thankfully, I wasn't in a complete state of undress when the poor plumber marched into the bedroom. I don't know who was the most embarrassed, but I noticed he didn't make eye contact with me for the rest of the time he was there. I couldn't believe David would just let the guy walk in, knowing that I was in there getting dressed. These days, I tend to give direct instructions to David and never make assumptions, but I don't always remember to do so. It doesn't feel right, especially if someone else is there to witness it.

Dream Holiday

As the build had dragged on longer than intended, it overlapped with a holiday we had planned with close friends to Florida. It was a very welcome break for us and the children. It was our first time in America as a family and I worried how the children who were still quite young would cope with the long nine-hour flight. I needn't have worried. They made use of the inflight entertainment and had their Nintendo games to hand. They were very well behaved. I on the other hand was going batty. I obsessively watched the screen that showed where the plane was and it just seemed like it was hardly moving at all!

We were shattered by the time we landed at the airport but still had to find our luggage and collect our hire cars. David, who was used to travelling by himself but not so much with family and particularly not with friends, just marched off without saying a word and we all had to run to keep up with him. I know he just wanted to get the car sorted and find the accommodation but he made no concessions for me, the kids or our friends.

The first park we visited was Disney's Magic Kingdom. The kids were so excited and awed by their surroundings. We decided as a group that we would stick together for the day and the first ride of choice was the Black Hole. James was holding my hand as we approached the ride, which was concealed inside a large building but he started to drag his feet and say he didn't want to go on it. I told him not to be silly and that it would be fun but he had already heard that the ride was in the dark and was getting very anxious. Everyone else was running ahead and I was having to drag him along. As we lined up in a thankfully short, moving

152

queue as we were there just after opening time, he started to cry.

By the time our car arrived and everyone else had found their seats he was hysterical. A member of staff insisted we would have to leave and ushered us through a hidden side door. What a disappointment. At the time, I had felt that if I could just get him on he would have been fine, but with more experience now I realise I was wrong and I would have compounded any issues he already had. That set the tone for the day. He hardly went on any rides and I spent most of my time sitting on benches with him whilst everyone else enjoyed exciting experiences like the Tower of Terror. It didn't occur to David to offer to share the burden with me.

At the house, James was happy as there was a pool, video games, lots of lovely junk food and friends he knew well. He was content.

We also visited the other Disney parks and in fact, James really enjoyed Epcot and the car test track. He even got up on stage in the Velcro exhibition with his sister to take part in a game show. That really surprised me.

David was most looking forward to Universal Studios as it was less whimsical and more relevant to us as adults and film lovers. We went on the old-fashioned ET flying adventure and the Jurassic Park boat ride which was thrilling. The ride David most wanted to go on was the Men in Black shooting drive but he started having a meltdown when he found out James was refusing to go in the building. We ended up having an argument because I said I would sit outside while he went in with Cathryn but he refused and I told him he was cutting his nose off to spite his face. We had come all this way and were right outside and he wouldn't go in!

153

James was sitting on the bench in the blazing sunshine whilst we argued above him when he spoke up. He said tearily, "This is all my fault isn't it.

My heart went out to him. He was having a moment of self-awareness and I paused before I answered him. I sat down next to him and decided not to lie. I gently said that yes, we were arguing because he was refusing to join in with the family fun. We had come such a long way and wanted all of us to join in together. James thought about this for a while and then took a deep breath and decided to be brave and go on the ride with us. I was so proud of him. We queued up and though he was very nervous and there were a few moments in the long queue where I thought he might make a run for it! He stayed and joined in the shooting the aliens ride. He had quite an enjoyable experience but he was little upset that he didn't 'win'.

We had a great few days and because I didn't think we would get the chance to go to America again, we came home via New York. This involved a short internal flight. We decided not to hire a car for our stay but use the less stressful transport modes of trains and taxis.

David's demeanour changed when we got to New York. He was overtly anxious as we had the children with us. I think his only information about the Big Apple was from cop shows. But we found it very safe and the people extremely friendly.

So, on the face of it you would think that going for a city break to one of the most exciting places in the world would be wondrous. Except that it wasn't. I felt that we didn't ever follow through on anything. We showed the kids where the Empire State Building was as it was on our block but we didn't go in it as someone at David's work had told him it wasn't the best place to get a view of New York.

We wanted to see the Statue of Liberty but David had read you could go on the ferry ride across the Hudson and get to see it that way. We did this and the ferry was packed with commuters and was quite some distance away from the statue. It just felt disappointing and anti-climactic.

We went to Central Park and watched people ice skating but when I asked if anyone wanted to go on, no one did. I would have loved a proactive husband who was keen to get up close and personal with people and activities instead of skirting around the edges of everything. Yes, we were there but did we really experience the atmosphere?

Despite my misgivings, before we knew it, it was time to come home. We came back to reality and an unfinished house with a bump.

Love and Loss

After the unsettling period of the build work was over, I discussed with David the possibly of getting another dog. He knows how much I love dogs and I felt it would be good for the kids and the family as a whole. He told me that it was fine as long as I didn't expect him to look after it. That was never an issue. So I found a breeder of Welsh springer spaniels in Yorkshire and we went a chose Bronwen. She came home to Northumberland at eight weeks old. The children and I were in love and David couldn't help being fond of her too.

Having a dog is a great socialiser and good for your health. It gets you out on walks whether you want to or not and people in the street always talk to you, especially with such a cute puppy. Bronwen was very popular in the school yard and as she got older we would regularly join other parents and dog walkers on popular walks in the village. She was a very loving and sociable dog. She was even quite obedient for a Welsh springer. I was able to let her off the lead along country roads and she would come and sit at my heels when a car came past.

We'd had her about a year when I popped into the vets in Hexham to book her an appointment for her boosters. The vets surgery is very close to Tyne Green, so while we were there I took Brownen for a quick walk. She was happily bounding around with a black Labrador and I was talking to its owner, another parent. I looked around wondering where my dog had got to and was just about to call her when a taxi drove fast down the lane beside the green. At that moment Bronwen ran out of a hedge after a bird and got hit by the speeding car. She was thrown up in the air, yelped and landed with a thud! I'd never run so fast in my life. I got to her just in time to see her draw her last breath. Her muzzle was bloodied and she was dead.

The taxi driver got out of his car and tried to make excuses. I couldn't talk to him. I just wanted my lovely puppy back. She was only fourteen months old and only just fully grown. Some very kind workmen picked her up for me and carried her back to my car. I still couldn't quite believe what had happened and so drove around the corner to the vets. I got a young vet to come out and check her, just in case. He confirmed to me in his gentle Scottish accent that she was gone. He offered to take her body but I wouldn't let him. I drove home, stunned.

It was a drizzly day while I dug a hole in the back garden for my beautiful pup. I dug as deep as I could until I was exhausted and hyperventilating and then gently laid her in, covered her in a cloth and put her bowl and lead in with her. It felt so disloyal to cover her up and leave her there but I did. I knew I had to before the children came home from school.

David was in Aberdeen when I rang him. I told him Bronwen had been hit by a car and he asked if she was alright.

"No! She'd dead!" I cried down the 'phone. He was shocked and didn't know what to say.

I had to pick Cathryn up from school and was dreading it. By the time I got there though, somehow everyone knew what had happened. I couldn't speak. I walked Cathryn home who chatted to me cheerfully. When we got in she asked,

"Where's Bronwen?"

I casually replied, "Oh, she's in the garden."

Cathryn didn't question it. I waited anxiously until James arrived home from middle school before I sat the children down and told them what had happened. Cathryn immediately burst into tears and James started laughing at his sister. I hadn't expected that reaction at all. I comforted Cathryn and let James go off to play on his computer. I was worried about him.

It was the end of the summer term and that was a school concert that evening. I took Cathryn back after tea and she ran to tell her friends the terrible news. They all gasped and put their arms around her. It was just what she needed.

The following morning, I drove James to school. He was sitting in the seat next to me and as we approached the school | I noticed there were tears pouring down his face. I realised it had taken him this long to process the death of our beloved dog. He always turned and said goodbye to her at this point and now she wasn't there. It had finally hit him.

After a week, David told me he was fed up of my moping around and that I should get another dog. I was surprised. In his gruff way, he was actually being sympathetic. Underneath he did care. I hadn't felt ready at all to replace Bronwen, but somehow David giving me permission to move on, made me feel it was okay to at least look.

I quickly found another breeder, in Yorkshire again. I rang to ask when the puppies would be ready, assuming it would be a few weeks but she said they were ready to go and we could come down any time! I was a bit shocked but David persuaded me that we should go and look. He drove back down to Yorkshire. I had very mixed feelings about this journey. I felt so guilty and disloyal to Bronwen but at the same time, excited. Who doesn't want to go and see puppies?

We arrived at the farm and were shown into the barn where ten little puppies were running around. The breeder asked me what kind of temperament I was looking for. After the very social and excitable Bronwen, I asked for a quiet one. She picked up two extremely cute pups and I had the quandary of choosing. I picked the one with the biggest eyes.

Maddi has been my constant companion for the last eight years. She is always at my side or my feet and sleeps in a basket in the bedroom. She only has eyes for me. It's good for the soul to have that unwavering loyalty.

Tolerance

In September 2008, Cathryn was started Reception and James moved up to Year Four. The teachers soon realised that she was the more reliable child at the age of four than James was at the age of eight, and they would trust Cathryn to bring home the school letters without losing them. Her Reception teacher said to me at her first parents evening that Cathryn was like James, but she talked!

As it was James's last year at first school it was a difficult period for him. His teachers started to report that he was crying a lot in class and he wouldn't tell them why. It was disrupting his work and sometimes the rest of the class. His teacher was very kind but she thought he was over-tired and suggested he got more sleep. He did often have trouble getting to sleep and would wander through to us on an evening, when he was meant to be in bed, just for a cuddle. He had dark shadows under his eyes. We tried to impose a stricter bedtime regime and to try and stop him from reading so late into the night.

James had been having terrible tummy problems for a while and was often constipated. I was convinced at the time that it was because he didn't eat enough fruit and vegetables. He had quite a self-restricted diet of pasta, pizza and chicken nuggets and sandwiches. I would try to get him to eat a more varied diet but it was a losing battle.

He would also have occasional 'accidents' where he didn't get to the toilet on time. This was because he spent too much time on the PlayStation and not enough time listening to his own body. I would get cross with him when I discovered the soiled underwear that he would hide away so as not to get into trouble.

160

For some years, I had been regularly attending clinics at the RVI in Newcastle in ophthalmology and neurology. They had still not worked out what my eye problems were related to. I was a bit of an enigma. Over the years I had been sent for IMRI scans, CT scans, lumbar punctures and muscle biopsies. My neurologist suspected I may have been in the early stages of multiple sclerosis but he couldn't prove it. None of the tests came back positive but there had been some anomalies on my IMRI scan that they couldn't explain. I was often still very tired and regularly suffered from painful migraines. However, in the end the neurologist decided he couldn't do anything more for me and I was discharged.

About this time, I went for a test at an alternative health clinic. I had been wondering for a while if I was wheat-intolerant and though I was sceptical about the growing trend of intolerances, I saw this as a last resort to sort my own health out. I was very lethargic and irritable a lot of the time. In a double-blind test, I was told that I was intolerant to wheat, dairy, parsnips and leeks. To be honest I was genuinely amazed as apart from liking most wheat-based products I had never liked milk, absolutely hated parsnips and had never been fond of leeks either. Other than those three things, apart from melon, I didn't have any absolute food dislikes. I was somewhat convinced there was something in it.

I can't deny I was a little daunted at first but I made the decision immediately to make changes to my diet. I started by cutting out all bread and wheat products. I stopped using cow's milk and changed to goat's milk when I could, or soya, though none of these alternatives were particularly palatable and I didn't feel any additional benefit from using them. I lost almost half a stone in weight very quickly and started feeling more energised, clear-headed and generally a nicer, less moody person. After a few weeks of not eating wheat and dairy I was tempted by hunger in a moment of weakness to have a chocolate chip cookie. I immediately began to feel quite fuzzy headed, irritable, windy and my eyesight was affected. I was cross with myself for being so weak-willed but it also proved to me that I was genuinely affected by these foods. Staying off them meant I was a more productive and tolerant person to be around.

It slowly dawned on me that James may also be wheat-intolerant as he loved typical children's food of pizza, pasta, bread and biscuits. I decided to change his diet too. I knew that he was very unhappy and feeling poorly a lot of the time and hoped he would be keen to try some food elimination. I had a grown-up conversation with him where I explained to him how much better I was feeling and how I hoped to help his tummy too. We agreed on a trial period of one week and he wasn't daunted by that. He readily agreed to it and never complained about missing his usual favourite foods.

The result was dramatic. Within a couple of days, he had much more energy and by the end of the week, the dark circles under his eyes had disappeared and he was a generally happier child. My main concern was the fact he had not had a bowel movement all week and I was starting to worry about him, that maybe I had been too stringent with this new diet. Thankfully after a week he did the most enormous solid poo in the toilet.

His teachers noticed the change in him and things improved in school for a while. As the year wore on though, James again began to show signs of stress and upset and we wondered again if he was worried about his impending move to middle school. His headteacher spoke to me and we requested contact with the educational psychologist. Again, nothing happened before he left.

In the September, James started middle school in the larger village nearby, with most of his First School classmates. Because of this his daily routine completely changed. He had to leave the house at eight in the morning and cross the busy main road in the village to get to where the children congregated. He was daunted by this journey to school alone, though I did arrange for him to walk with another child from his class which helped for a while until we discovered this child was bullying him. It was not the done thing for your parent to walk you to the bus stop though I think he would have been so much happier if I had.

At first, I thought his move to middle school had gone reasonably well, but we were brought to earth with a thump when his form teacher told me at a parents' evening in October that James was, "The most awkward child I've ever had to teach". I was devastated. According to this so-called professional; he didn't listen, he was disorganised and he was disruptive in class. He would cry and then refuse to tell the teacher what the problem was. It never occurred to her that he couldn't, not wouldn't.

For the second time in a year I agreed to meet with the educational psychologist. This time she was called in as a priority. The meeting started off with James' form teacher and the school special educational needs coordinator (SENCo), telling the educational psychologist what a difficult child he was. I was astounded by her insensitivity. David did not accompany me as he was working and he did not like to get involved with anything to do with school unless he had to.

Thankfully, James's form teacher left the room so that I could have a private talk with the educational psychologist. Sarah was quite young but calm and listened carefully while I voiced my concerns about my nine-year old son. I had come prepared and had written a list of reasons why. As I had typed up my list and saved the file I have inserted it below:

Notes on James

James's problems as we see them:

Highly sensitive often thinks he is in the wrong, even when he isn't
Needs constant reassurance of affection

Can be quite shy

Does not like loud noises, will avoid if possible *e.g. left school disco and went to ICT room for afternoon.*

Does not like to try new things in case of failure

Probably worries a lot about things but does not communicate this

Is an easy target for bullies

Tunnel vision - can often seem like he is in a world of his own

Does not notice or acknowledge things or people he is not interested in. This can come across as very rude, but it isn't deliberate. *I never let him get away with this, although his paternal grandmother thinks that it is fine.*

Organisation - Finds it very hard to organise and prioritise. *We do our best to make sure he has everything he needs for school but often homework does not get handed in.*

Constantly forgets and loses things. *Having lost at least everything once, all his possessions are labelled several times. This does help the recovery rate somewhat.*

Physically - Quite often has difficulty getting to sleep.

Was a terrible sleeper as a baby

Often has tummy problems and diarrhoea

Suspected wheat intolerance - waiting for assessment

James's Good Points

- Academically very bright
- Inquisitive, questioning mind
- Enjoys reading very much
- Has a good sense of humour
- Can be surprisingly confident about public speaking
- Has a good retentive memory
- Will talk at length about subjects he is interested in
- Wants to please
- Very loving
- Has made some good friendships
- Gets on very well with his sister

Reasons We Think James Is Like This – Family Background

- It runs in both sides of the family!
- Both David and I are naturally shy people
- James's father David is a unique and talented individual. As far as I can tell from conversations with his mother he was a highly intelligent child who could turn his hand to most things. He built his first computer (with some help from his father) at the age of 11. David works extremely hard in his chosen field and is a perfectionist and workaholic.
- My eldest brother is also very bright and successful, but at the age of 6 sent by his infant school see an educational psychologist. He could

be a difficult child needing reassurance, quite often in a world of his own. He was never on time for anything and his high school just accepted this.

James As a Young Child

- Was very clingy
- Did not sleep *(for two years!)*
- Was very interested in what was happening around him
- Loved books
- Loved typical boy things but did not get on with more boisterous children
- Would spend hours setting up train track and playing intricate games with trains
- Would overreact to the slightest hurt. *Could not tell if stubbed toe or had leg chopped off.*
- Had severe tantrums from 18 months to the age of three
- Had night terrors and nightmares

As parents, we have discovered that James needs patience, understanding and attention from us but since we are still learning what makes James tick we are not surprised that some of James's teachers are a little puzzled by him.

The educational psychologist spent five minutes carefully reading through what I had written and then she turned to me and gently said that what I had written was very useful and showed evidence that my son had either autism or Asperger Syndrome. I was shocked but not surprised. I felt myself shaking at the thought of my son having this diagnosis. All I knew about autism was what you occasionally saw in the press of uncontrollable children or savants portrayed in films like Rainman. I looked at her and said, "What's Asperger Syndrome?"

She explained it was a type of higher-functioning autism and suggested I go away and read up on Asperger Syndrome (AS), and in the meantime James would be referred to the local Children's Mental Health Service (CAMHS).

Revelation

With some trepidation, I bought Tony Attwood's 'Complete Guide to Asperger Syndrome'. I approached it with an open mind, not knowing what to expect. I didn't know if I wanted it to make sense or whether I could turn around after reading up on Asperger Syndrome and say, 'This has nothing to do with my son.' Deep down, I knew James needed help and so I started reading. Usually, given a text book I'll flick or skip through chapters until I find something interesting. This book I read from cover to cover with barely a break.

However, it started to dawn on me as I read it that not only was the author talking about my son but I started to identify other members of my family. I read the chapter on relationships and it could have been written about me and David. I found tears pouring down my face as I recognised my husband's behaviours within our marriage. I think I also felt relief to know that I was not alone. That I wasn't going mad and that there was a reason for the way he treated me and the children.

But like the 'Cat in the Hat', that was not all. In the chapter on women with Asperger's' I recognised the peculiar habits of my late, paternal grandmother. Her eccentricities, obsessions, the way she was so rude, picky, pedantic, squirreled away food and would never stay for long. I started to recognise these traits, not just in my husband and son but in my side of the family too. If my grandmother had been an undiagnosed woman with Asperger Syndrome her eccentricities made sense, but also my childhood and my difficult relationship with my father. As I read further, I recognised more traits as Tony Attwood pointed out these children would often be known as little professors. I gasped as I remembered my elder brother Rhys had had such difficulties in Infant School, being bright but considered rude and awkward. In high school the teachers had a soft spot for him and called him 'Professor'.

All of this fell in to place as I avidly devoured this new bible. I knew that Sarah had been right and now I needed to learn to accept this deluge of enlightenment and information. The next and hardest task was to speak to my husband and try and explain to him that he may be autistic.

I wasn't even convinced it was autism. I could just about believe it was this 'Asperger's Syndrome'. In a way, it was up to him to make this conclusion. At first, I could tell he didn't want to be labelled with some 'quack's' mumbo-jumbo, but the more we talked about it in the context of James, also the more David opened up to me about his childhood. There were so many things he had never told me before. How he was bullied at school, how he felt different from his peers growing up and stories about his own father's behaviour.

Support

In the meantime, I had been to visit my GP and while I was there, I asked if he knew of any local support groups for parents of autistic children. He didn't have a clue. I was very disappointed and despondent. I desperately needed to talk to someone about my child who understood what I was going through. When I got home from the surgery I started searching on the internet. I soon found to my surprise that a National Autistic Society group was being set up in Hexham by local parents. I had missed their first meeting but the article in the *Hexham Courant* mentioned a further gathering at the high school.

I dragged a reluctant husband with me. I was apprehensive and needed his support. We entered a classroom with many other parents and waited for the meeting to start. A couple of people had brought children with them and I couldn't help looking at them curiously, wondering if they were autistic. They looked fine to me. One boy was industriously working with crayons and loudly asking his dad questions. I was a little jealous of the father/son interaction. It wasn't until I observed interactions like this, that it brought it home to me how little David connected with his children.

The organisers gave an introductory talk about autism and why they thought Hexham needed a support group, and what the NAS could do for families with autism in our area. Much of the discussion was about children with severe autism and what help they could get. They discussed the possibility of getting a grant for a facility within the High School for autistic children to take part in mainstream education. Though I thought this was great, at the time I could tell that David felt very uncomfortable about the discussion.

He had surprised me by being open to the possibility of having Asperger Syndrome, which is looked upon almost positively compared to classic autism. I could tell he was feeling very uncomfortable at being considered 'autistic'. So far, there had been no mention of Asperger Syndrome, and I was starting to wonder if we were in the wrong place. The discussion moved on and towards the end of the evening people started to discuss Asperger's. I felt David relax a little. This he could cope with.

I managed to speak to a few parents and surprised myself by feeling quite tearful when discussing James with them. They were understanding and kind and told me about the monthly support meetings. I hadn't realised quite how much emotion I had been hiding from myself, let alone everyone else.

As the meetings were during the day, David could not come along, but I don't think they were for him anyway. I was the one who needed emotional support. I gave my all at home to my family and I needed to find like-minded people. David got all the support he needed from me.

The first support group I attended I didn't know what to expect but was greeted warmly by two friendly women and a young couple. I was made coffee and introduced to everyone and then given time to tell my story. There were a lot of questions, interjections and understanding. Some of what they talked about went over my head. They asked if I had a statement for my child and when I said 'No,' they tried to tell me how to go about getting one. This all felt a bit much but it was difficult to say to them that I didn't believe my son needed a statement. I knew what he needed most of all was understanding from his school, which he was not getting at the time.

I discovered that the parents at the support group had children of varying severity on the autistic spectrum. One of the mums had multiple children on the spectrum which I could not comprehend. How did she cope? I was just about managing with my little family.

The young couple had a son who was statemented but were having tremendous struggles with him and his current school. Even though it was all a bit bewildering I came away from those first couple of hours uplifted. I had been listened to and more to the point, believed. People knew what struggles I was going through without me having to spell it out and they asked me the right questions and gave offers of support and advice which I had never received before.

I started attending these meetings as often as I could. I would mention them to David and he seemed pleased that I was going. I got to know more mums and as we began to see each other regularly. We became better than acquaintances and more like friends.

I still go for much needed support, information sharing, laughter, validation and reciprocation. My role has changed into a more advisory capacity these days but I still benefit from it.

Assessment

I was envious of those with a diagnosis for their child but soon we were contacted by the local CAMHS team regarding James and I took him along for his first appraisal. Again, I did not know what to expect. We met with a nurse and nurse manager who talked to me while James was there. For the next few sessions, I took James alone and we met up with the nurse. At one appointment, Susan asked James if he would make a collage of his interests to show her for the next appointment. James agreed to do it but it was very hard to make him start on it. It took several hours of coaxing and idea-forming to come up with.

Shortly before his next session with Susan, the session was cancelled. The appointment was rescheduled for a few days later. When we went in to see Susan she told us that James would not be under her care anymore as she was moving back to Morpeth. She did not at any stage ask to see the collage that James and I had worked so hard on. This was disappointing. I felt confused, so how was James feeling? What kind of example did this attitude from professionals set to my son who didn't understand people at the best of times?

In discussion with my NAS group shortly after, they were not surprised. For some time, the atmosphere in our local CAMHS had been terrible with a high staff turnover. This was a terrible situation for any medical service but especially one in mental health and autism where the children needed consistency and continuity of care.

I would report all these happenings back to David but he basically left the responsibility to me and we never discussed the situation in any detail as it would only stress him out. He stuck to what he knew; working hard and bringing money in.

It was a difficult and frustrating time for us as a family but eventually after waiting some months, James was invited to see an occupational therapist called Anna. Anna was wonderful with James and spent time talking to and observing him. I had to sit and wait, twiddling my thumbs as I didn't know what they were doing. When Anna came out she told me that James perfectly and rather unusually, fit the 'Triad of Impairment'. She seemed quite astonished by this as if she had rarely come across such a prime example. I smiled as if I knew what she was talking about but didn't have a clue what the 'Triad of Impairment' was. I went home and looked it up.

Anna also came for a home visit. She wanted to know what James was like in his natural environment. James was quite happy that she was there. He had never minded people coming into our home. We set up a board game for him and Cathryn to play. When James lost to his sister he was a typical bad loser. I noticed Anna making notes while he was having a strop. Cathryn was perfectly behaved as usual. My little star. It didn't for one moment cross my mind that she might be on the spectrum too.

As part of her support, Anna went into the middle school to observe James in a classroom environment. I was quite envious and I wished I could be a fly on the wall too. Anna reported back that she was quite shocked to see how badly he coped with lessons. She told me how he had difficulty with a change in routine and that she was lucky enough to observe this on this day. She had been observing during his maths lesson where he taken a while to settle in. He hadn't had the equipment he needed but once the teacher sorted him out he had settled down.

This happened to be the day the whole school were having their photographs taken and the lesson was soon disrupted by the children being asked to troop to the hall to wait in line for the photographer. Anna said it was clear that James had no clue what was happening, or why it was happening. He was looking around confused that the lesson had abruptly ended.

She observed him being quite distressed and that he continued to be for some time after. The staff seemed unaware of why he would be distressed or how to calm him.

Anna knew our son needed help, but first he needed an official diagnosis, or the school would not take any positive action.

I don't know whether Anna had any influence but we quickly got to see a consultant psychologist, Dr Victoria Thomas. This time, David came to the appointment as we were told parental input was very important. The appointment was in the usual building in Hexham and James came in quietly, wouldn't take his coat off and sat slumped in the chair with no eye-contact. The consultant was very easy to talk to and friendly. She explained the process clearly and spent time talking to us. Dr Thomas asked a lot of questions about James as a baby. Much of that time is an exhaustive blur but I answered as well as I could.

It was easier to answer questions about his current behaviour. One question that sticks in my mind was when she asked,

"How does James react if he comes home from school and you have moved the furniture around?"

I laughed and said that James wouldn't even notice but I pointed to his father and said,

"He would freak out. I've learned not to do that."

By the end of two hours, James was bored to death and we were emotionally drained. The consultant hinted broadly that we would be getting the diagnosis that we needed. It was such a relief to hear this. Soon after, we received the official confirmation that James had Asperger Syndrome. It was both a relief and a punch in the stomach to get the official confirmation. I had a child with a disability.

Now he had an official diagnosis the school was obliged to take action. David would attend some of the meetings with me as I felt at first it would be helpful. Only sometimes his presence made it much worse. He would be defensive and argumentative towards the teachers. My tactic was to listen to them and work with them and correct them and give them advice when needed but he did not see it like that. At times, he made me uncomfortable and embarrassed.

Anna arranged to have a meeting at James's middle school with the SENCo, head of year and us. After a difficult and depressing meeting, we walked outside quietly. Anna had not been to this school before. She could not believe the opposition that we were up against from the staff. She turned to us and asked whether we had considered moving him to another school. We admitted we had thought about it but that would make life difficult for James, taking him away from his friends and into another new environment. We had decided it was 'better the devil you know'.

In a later meeting with the SENCo and headteacher, Anna offered the staff training, and once the headteacher realised that the training would be free, she almost took Anna's hand off.

In the meantime, Anna had again visited James in school. Together they drew a 'schoologram' where he could tell her in diagrammatical form how he felt about his lessons and what would improve them for him. For instance, he said he liked to sit near the door so he could get out first without being bumped and barged and to be able to sit where he could see a clock so he knew how long the lesson had to go. This would stop him worrying and help him to concentrate on the lesson. This 'schoologram' was passed on to the staff who read it and some of them found it very useful to try and understand what James was going through every day. This made a huge difference to his last two years at middle school. We have a lot to thank Anna for.

I continued to drive James into school until he left in July 2012. His transition to high school which the newly aware middle school staff had worked hard on was initially very successful.

Eruption

After our successful trip to Florida 2008 we planned another, longer holiday there. We booked for two weeks. We had had a falling out with Virgin Holidays, who had managed to lose any details of our flights which we had booked well in advance. In the end we had to drive a hire car to Glasgow and fly to Orlando from there and our return flight was to Gatwick and then onwards to Newcastle. Our friends flew out from Manchester and arrived a few hours before us.

I was feeling quite run down, despite the fact we were really looking forward to our long Easter holiday. I had a debilitating cough that had hung around for weeks. It made having a conversation really difficult. Thankfully within a few days of arriving my cough disappeared. It was either coincidence or the warm weather. The first week was fantastic as we spent more time going to the water parks and doing things we hadn't done before. Towards the end of the second week though we started to hear rumours that there might be problems getting home. A volcano had erupted in Iceland and the cloud of ash was so bad that flights were being grounded for safety reasons. We weren't too worried at first, thinking there were still a few days to go before the end of our holiday but the more we investigated we found out that our flights home had been cancelled.

We went and found the holiday reps. who were less than helpful. They had hundreds of worried people to deal with who were staying in hotels and running out of money. All they said was that we were on a list and would be called when the flights started again. We went through a range of emotions; the first being shock and worry, the second was an unexpected extension to a wonderful holiday.

178

Bradley was proactive and contacted the house owners and found out that the house wasn't due to be let out again for another fortnight. They were quite happy for us to stay longer, as long as we paid for it of course. That was a big relief.

As our 'holiday' extended, David became increasingly concerned about the work he had left at home. He had brought his laptop, so he was able to do a little bit but every day we spent there meant he wasn't really earning anything and it was costing us a lot in accommodation, car hire, activities and food. He was becoming increasingly short tempered not just with me but also with the children and a couple of times I caught him being quite short with our friend's son, Harry which it was not his place to do.

On the whole, we rubbed along quite well together. There were eight of us in a five bedroom house with pool. The children were quite happy and got along well and were not at all bothered about missing school. For us adults and particularly for David, it was the uncertainty of what was going to happen that was the problem.

On our first two weeks of official holiday, we had visited most of the parks that we had wanted to. We had of course budgeted for the astronomical amount this would cost us but now we found ourselves staying more in the house, waiting for the 'phone to ring. To our delight we discovered that the park owners of Universal and Disney announced that if we could show we were stranded we could visit their parks for free. Since the parks had quickly realised that due to no flights landing in Florida they were well down on visitors and takings. They also realised that for most of the stuck holiday makers that this was a once in a lifetime holiday which would have been saved and budgeted for. No one could afford to pay the park prices twice. The parks still had to pay their staff and knew that if they opened the parks for free at least the tourists would be buying food and toys. It was a good move for everyone. This way we had something to do during the day and they at least would have visitors who would still spend money.

We took full advantage of this, though I have to say, it was nowhere near as exciting visiting Universal for the second time. It was a surreal experience, especially as you never know if your phone would go and you'd be called to get on a flight. We were living out of packed suitcases and didn't know whether to shop for food or not. I remember mentioning to David it was like being in the film, Groundhog Day, doing the same thing day after day with no way of escape.

After ten days, things came to a head. We had seen on the news that planes were starting to fly again but there was a huge backlog to get all the stranded holiday makers home. We had heard on the grapevine that some Virgin customers had managed to get on flights home and Bradley decided he was going to go back to the airport and see if he could find someone else to talk to. David thought it was a waste of time and refused to go with him. I wasn't happy about this and was quite frustrated with his attitude.

Some hours later, Bradley came home beaming saying he had managed to speak to an official at the airport and he had managed to get his family on to a specially-commissioned flight. They started packing. It was gutting to see that they were suddenly leaving. David was cross because Bradley had also spoken to the rep. who said we would 'probably' get a phone call ourselves. This was no guarantee and we felt we were left in total limbo. The uncertainty was difficult for me, but excruciating for David.

To make matters worse, Bradley took it upon himself to ring up the owners of the house and tell them that they were leaving and they could send the cleaners in. David, who was at his laptop in the next room, overheard this conversation and to my horror started screaming at Bradley:

"What the fuck are you doing?"

Bradley was really taken aback at this. He had never seen the normally mild-mannered David angry before and he couldn't work out what he had done wrong. I tried to calm David down and take him out of the room but it didn't work. He just kept asking Bradley why he had made the phone call. Lisa came in horrified to find out what all the noise was about.

The atmosphere was terrible but Lisa and Bradley continued to pack so they would get their flight that afternoon. David was now terrified that we would not get a flight and that now we wouldn't have a roof over our head. I managed to calm David down enough to convince him he needed to go to the airport and try and talk to someone, preferably the same official Bradley had got hold of. I said I would contact him if we received a phone call about the flight.

David drove off and I was left in the house with Lisa and Bradley. I can't remember what was said. I know Lisa asked if I was okay. I probably said "Yes," but I really wasn't. I was shell-shocked by David's complete meltdown. Yet, in some ways I had been expecting it sooner, though not as explosive or aimed at Bradley. David did completely over-react but he was put in such a situation of uncertainty where he was trying to hold it all together in a foreign country where the talk was that we would be stuck for months. He tells me now that if it had just been him he would have been fine, but the added responsibility of his young family was just too much for him.

Then for the situation to be taken totally out of his hands and the thought of being without a roof over our heads and nowhere to go was too much for him.

As it was, David eventually rang me from the airport to say he had managed to get us on a flight that afternoon and to start packing. We had to throw all the food out and hurriedly pack all the suitcases and jump into the car the moment David got back. We ended up being on the same flight as our friends but we did not travel together. We never thought this would happen to us but I don't think any of us knew how to handle the situation. It was a terrible journey home, especially as the plane we were on was ready for the scrap-yard. We weren't bothered that there was no in-flight entertainment or the cramped seating, but we were bothered by the huge amount of creaking and the aviation fumes. There was an enormous cheer as we landed finally at Heathrow.

Arriving back in Blighty was not the end of the problems. Most people on the flight had actually landed at completely the wrong airport. Our friends had to make their way back to Manchester to pick up their car. We were meant to have flown into Gatwick and then back up to Newcastle – if we had come home on the right date but that date was almost two weeks previously. Fortunately, this is where there are certain advantages to being married to an Aspie. David had kept the whole paper trail of disaster the whole way from being messed about with our outbound flights to our dreadful postponed and cramped flight home, arriving at the wrong airport and also an item of luggage damaged. I was completely shattered and David left me with the luggage to and two tired children while he went to talk to the Virgin staff. Before we knew it we were being escorted by a helpful young man who bought us tickets to get the bus to the correct airport and even helped us on to the right bus. Virgin had even paid for our flights to get home to Newcastle. All we had to do was follow instructions and get a taxi home from Newcastle airport.

The following few weeks were very awkward between our two families. Lisa and I did not stop speaking but I knew they were very upset with David's behaviour and the fact he had not apologised. David however, still could not understand Bradley's actions and felt justified in his reaction. Thankfully, David eventually realised that he did not want to lose their friendship and maybe he even realised how difficult it was making life for me and my best friend. After a lot of consideration, he sent an e-mail explaining why he had reacted the way he did and apologised in it. We are now good friends again but no one had ever mentioned the idea of sharing a holiday again. The memory is too painful for all of us.

Tolerance has its Limits

I was researching on university websites for one of David's projects, when I got side-tracked by the courses in the Northumbria University prospectus. I came across a Master's degree course in Autism and read it with interest, wondering what professionals would be learning to deal with people like my family members. The course content seemed interesting and relevant. I was jealous of the students on this course. Then at the end of the course information I spotted that this was also open to parents.

I was intrigued. Could I do this? This would help me so much and give me ammunition when I had to deal with the school dragging its heels. I would be able to stand my ground and fight for my child's rights with confidence. I decided I had nothing to lose and applied. I didn't for one moment believe that I would be accepted on to the course. My main concern, if they accepted me, was how was the workload but I thought I would cross that bridge when I came to it. I rang the university to find out how much commitment it would be. It was one evening a week for three years. I felt I could handle that.

I didn't mention it to my friends as I expected to be rejected, but a few weeks later I was astounded to receive a letter in the post confirming my unconditional place.

Gaslighting

It was just before Christmas and I was very aware how stressed he was getting with the coming seasons festivities coming up. My father was visiting with his new girlfriend, though thankfully not staying with us and as usual, David felt

184

the pressure of having to buy me a present and not knowing what I would want. Despite telling him I was fine without much for Christmas, as a Christmas present for me would be him in a festive mood and not ruining the atmosphere, he would not accept this. This came out in angry rants every now and then.

We were in the study together at our separate desks, when I noticed a post on Facebook from a friend who had taken a much-wanted redundancy package. I made the mistake of remarking on this. Afterwards, the insanity of the conversation rang so clearly in my head I quickly typed it up before I forgot it or convinced myself that it hadn't happened.

I casually mentioned over my shoulder, "I see Paul is taking redundancy."

David replied from his desk behind me, "That's a funny time to be taking it."

I answered back, "Well I think he can turn his hand to anything."

He turned in his chair and snarled, "So, what you mean is, that I need to get a job!"

I was completely taken aback by this attitude that had seemed to come out of nowhere. Rather irritated, I said forcefully, "No, you've got a job."

Then I sat there quietly wondering what on earth was going on in his head.

April Fool!

Six months in, my course was going well. I found it hard work but invigorating. I was learning a great deal about my family and my husband and why they acted in the way they did. I got a lot of validation and understanding from our seminars and discussions on a Thursday night. I felt my confidence growing a little.

It was April 1st, 2011, and I had an assignment due in soon. I dropped my daughter off at school and joined some friends on a dog walk in the woods. On the way, back down a steep slope I got distracted by a bug flying into my raincoat and as I flapped it to get it out I didn't notice a set of steps set into the hillside. As I fell I flung my arm out to save myself and ended up smacking my right elbow on the step. My friend stopped and asked if I was hurt. I thought I'd knocked my funny bone and other than losing my dignity I was fine. I managed to catch the dog and stroll back to the car I'd left outside the school. For some reason, I couldn't manage to open the door on the first attempt. Still, I got the dog in and managed to drive the short distance home rather awkwardly.

I thought I would catch up with some college work and then I was expecting a friend was who wanted to go shopping. As I sat at my desk I watched my arm starting to swell. I took some ibuprofen and hoped that would fix it. After an hour and the pain relief was ineffective, I started to worry. When the doorbell rang, I let Fiona in and said rather miserably said that I didn't think we would be able to go shopping. I thought I had better go to casualty. She must have seen how pale I was and didn't for a second assume it was an April Fool. She drove me to Hexham and waited while I was examined. The young doctor examined me and asked me how much pain I was in out of ten. I had my arm folded across my chest and said I thought it was about a three. He took my arm and moved it towards him and I shrieked "Ten!".

I was sent to X-ray and it was confirmed I had a nasty elbow fracture. I really didn't need this! He assured me that it would be okay in about a month and that I would be able to drive again in six weeks.

Fiona had stayed with me the whole time and took me home again without complaint. I had texted David from X-ray but he hadn't come home any sooner. He was fairly sympathetic when he did arrive home and saw my arm in a sling. He made me a cup of coffee and went back to his desk.

Somehow, I managed to make the kids' tea with my one good arm and then I sat at my desk and contemplated how, with a break in my right elbow, I was going to manage to complete my assignment. I soon worked out that if I slipped my arm out of the sling I could still manipulate the mouse with my right hand.

I made the mistake of trying to carry on as usual, so once David realised that I could still make coffee, cook tea and walk the dog with only one arm he didn't see the need to help me with this burden.

The first morning after my accident, I asked him if he could help me get dressed. It's hard trying to do your bra up or pull your jeans on with one hand! I don't know who ended up the most traumatised. He didn't know how to help me without hurting me and got angry with me when I was directing him. I told him to stop and that I would do it by myself in future.

187

Fiona was an absolute godsend as I had already employed her to look after the kids for me on Thursday evenings when I attended university. She extended her hours and helped drive me places if I could guarantee that David would remember to pick the kids up from school and feed them too.

I didn't wait six weeks until I got back into the driver's seat. It ached a bit and I didn't dare tell my physio but I couldn't rely on my friends for ever and life didn't stop just because I'd broken my arm!

Road Rage!

We were also trying to organise and rearrange our life a little better. We had made the false economic mistake of not putting fitted wardrobes in to our dressing room but keeping the big old wooden wardrobes we had had for years. They didn't fit and it was hard to put clothes away. It was always a chore. Eventually I persuaded David that we needed to look at fitted wardrobes. He hated the idea of spending more money but agreed in principle. It turns out wardrobes are expensive! He suggested that we buy the parts ourselves and he would fit them. He is quite practical though I hate having to be his labour as he just shouts at me all the time and always expects me to clear up his mess and he is very messy!

We needed to get these enormous wardrobes into the storage units and that involved hiring a van. I found a family business run from a nearby farm that seemed good value. I booked the van and the following day we jumped in the car to go and collect it. To get to the farm we had to drive through the next village which has quite a convoluted one-way system and I noted that David had driven down the wrong road. I hesitated to mention it at first as I knew he hated to be criticised but I realised that we would end up going miles out of our way. After a moment's consideration, I started to point out in as neutral a way as I could, that we were going down the wrong road. He still got angry with me, verbally lashing out and making it seem like my fault. One of the hardest things about being an Asperger wife is that you never seem to work as a team. My pointing out his mistake should have actually helped the situation if he had acknowledged it. Instead he took it as a personal attack.

I then realised that there was a little short cut I had used once and that we could possibly follow that windy lane. To try and redeem the situation, I tried to tell him about this but this time he yelled,

"Do you want to drive?"

He's done this to me before but for once I was annoyed enough to call his bluff. I surprised him by saying I did and he pulled the car on to the verge. We crossly swapped places. There's only so much patience and tolerance I have before exploding. I'm very good at biting my tongue and walking away to avoid conflict, no matter how angry I am. There was no walking away and I was annoyed, as no matter what I did, or said, I was always in the wrong. I jumped in the car, strapped my seatbelt on, glanced down the empty road behind me and put my foot down. The little blue Clio made a very satisfying vroom noise as I sped off in the direction of the short cut. It went a long way to easing my annoyance at the unfair way he was treating me. What I didn't expect next was his reaction.

He started screaming, "Stop the car! Stop the Car! You're going to kill me!"

I couldn't' believe my ears. I had accelerated quickly but controlled manner and actually wasn't' going that fast but he decided I was driving dangerously. I thought it would be ridiculous to stop straightaway but he kept hanging on to his seat and screaming as if I was rallying the car. I saw the turning up ahead and pulled over. Calmly, I pointed out that if he wanted to, he could drive the rest of the way and this was the road I was trying to tell him about. We swapped seats again since apparently, I had a death wish. By the time we reached the farm, he had calmed enough to act as if nothing had happened but my adrenaline was still making me shake and wonder whether I could put up with this much longer.

The Best of Intentions

We were on a mission to tidy up our bungalow to put it up for sale. The estate agent was due the following day. David however, made it very clear that he would rather be in his office working; doing something productive. I was extremely motivated to move and was busy cleaning and occasionally asking for help with technical or heavy items. I had been careful not to wind him up and we had agreed in advance that David would set up the power washer that I needed to clean the garden paths. Typically, nothing is ever straightforward and a small but significant piece of the pressure washer had broken whilst wintering in the shed. I was reluctant at first to mention this as I knew what his reaction would be, but for the greater good I had to ask for help. David predictably became agitated as he knew I wanted the garden to be look perfect for the next day. As it was already Sunday afternoon it was not possible to get to the shops to buy a replacement part.

Though I was disappointed at the turn of events, I decided to use an ordinary garden hose and a stiff brush to get the job done. I proceeded to work on cleaning the paths whilst David spent over an hour searching for a replacement piece of equipment, cursing as he went. After some time, I realised I was having a noticeable effect on the paths and was starting to feel pleased with my work. The evening sun came out and dried out the paths, showing the improvements more clearly. I cheerfully called out to David that he should take a look at the garden. He made no comment. Instead, he began vigorously brushing the same area, intermittently shouting demands at me. By this time, I was at a height cleaning windows. I kept calm and gritted my teeth and deliberately complimented him upon his work but to no avail. Still he was in a bad mood.

After a time, he disappeared and I found him in the front yard manically hosing and brushing paving I had already cleaned. I pointed out that I had already done that but he started shouting at me loudly that it wasn't good enough and he thought I wanted it done! As it was such a lovely evening the street was quite busy with other neighbours also gardening and enjoying the rare sunshine. I was mortified and angry that he was treating me like that in front of the neighbours. I'd had enough.

I jumped in the car and roared off down the street. Only as I did so my mother in law drove past with the children in the back of the car. She looked rather surprised and all I could see were the big eyes of my children as I left. I drove to the end of the village and found somewhere quiet to park. I took a few minutes to calm down and then I returned. David was looking agitated and he and his mother had seemed to discuss the fact that I may have left. Linda decided not to stay around and normality resumed without us ever discussing his behaviour towards me.

Going Berserk

Most of the time I keep my cool but you never know what is going to be the straw that breaks the camel's back.

July 2011, it seemed I was under more stress than usual. I had an assignment due in and I was having great difficulty with it. Also, my dog, Maddi had injured herself badly on a walk and put pressure on one of her vertebrae. According to the vet she was within millimetres of becoming paralysed and I hadn't been allowed to walk her for two weeks. She was becoming quite difficult with pent-up energy as spaniels need a lot of walking.

This particular morning, it had been very difficult to get James to school and he had had a meltdown which had taken some dealing with. David had also been upset about something and was blaming me for it. I had to get Cathryn to school and dash home in time for a friend to pick me up as we were going to an NAS meeting. It was a lovely sunny day and I had walked Cathryn to school, taking Maddi for her first gentle stroll in a while.

As Maddi and I rounded the last grassy bend in our street before our bungalow, she insisted on doing the most enormous poo on the grass. This was something she never did as she was the most fastidious dog with her toileting habits. I was unable to stop her as she must have been desperate. In my haste to get Cathryn to school, I had not put any bags in my pocket but as we were nearly home I walked quickly down the street to my house. To my annoyance, we must have been observed by a neighbour, one who had moved in recently, who started banging on her window and shouting,

193

"Your dog's done a poo! Your dog's done a poo!"

This was blindingly obvious and in my heightened state I didn't acknowledge her. As is my habit after a dog walk, I took Maddi to the side gate and released her lead. Instead of her usual dash up the side of the house, the fed-up dog escaped through my legs and out into the street. She dashed straight in front of an oncoming car. My heart was in my mouth and my legs turned to jelly as we had lost our previous dog to a road accident. The car missed her by inches. I could really feel the tension rising as tracked Maddi into a neighbour's back garden. Trespassing, I managed to corner her and put her back on the lead. Just as we re-crossed the road I saw a woman I didn't recognise marching determinedly up the street towards me.

I knew immediately from her body language that this was the window-banger and that she wasn't happy with my actions. As she started haranguing me again, I put my hand out palm towards her and warned her,

"Don't start."

Well she didn't heed my warning and started to accuse me of giving dog owners a bad name and letting the street down. I was furious as I had lived in the street and village for many more years than her. I was particularly cross as she hadn't even given me a chance to get in the house and find a poop bag which had been my intention. I remember asking her if she expected me to pick it up with my bare hands and she informed me I should carry a bag with me 'at all times'!

I honestly don't remember what I said after that but I saw red and must have said exactly what I think. She has never approached me since. I have no idea whether I told her what a bad day/week/month/decade I was having.

Afterwards, my friend picked me up on time and just as we were driving away we saw Maddi yet again, escaping down the road. I had managed to leave both the back door and the gate wide open.

Breaking Point

My dad had invited himself along on our Tuscan holiday and at the time it seemed like a good idea to share the expense with him, and to give him a holiday now he had split up with his girlfriend. He drove up from West Wales to our house and we caught a flight from Newcastle airport to Pisa the next day. However, my poor dad was suffering badly from sciatica and could barely walk. Even though I carried his luggage, he was lagging behind. I could tell it was already irritating David.

When we had originally booked the flights with Jet2 they had been earlier in the day but they had changed the flight times to later which meant we would be arriving shortly before dark. This was not ideal as David and I had never been to Italy before. The outbound flight was fine, but by the time we had got through Italian customs and found the hire car place it was dark. It took us quite some time to find the car we had been allocated. Thankfully, we had set up the GPS in advance and had little difficulty finding our way to the mountainous area where our villa was. Yet in the pitch black it became impossible to find.

I was sitting in the back of the car with the kids to give my dad more leg-room. My dad kept playing with the air-conditioning and complaining about the music we had brought and I could tell David was trying very hard not to get annoyed. The road became excruciatingly narrow, with hairpin bends and we had no idea what the drop down the mountainside was like. Occasionally, local cars would come racing down towards us. David, who was obviously quite tired by this time, started shouting at me to look at the directions to try and find the house in the dark.

It was hard to read the directions in the back of the car and we ended up going down a wrong track but it took us a few minutes to realise it. Eventually we found what we thought was the right track but it was down a very steep unmade road with a sharp drop on the left-hand side. David started to panic as he was not convinced we were in the right place especially as the name on the gate was different to the one we had written down. However, there was nowhere to turn around so we had to carry on. In the dark, it was hard to see where the road ended.

David ended up doing a three-point turn just past the house. We were all worried that the car would plunge off the cliff. David was frantic and the children were scared. Once the car was turned around we got out. In the dark, I said to David that I thought it looked like the picture of the house I had seen on the internet and even though the name was different we were in the right area. He didn't think it was the right place. There was no one there to greet us but the key was in the front door and we could get in. David was still convinced we were in the wrong place but I refused to leave as it was nearly midnight. By this point I was so tired I was shaking and stubbornness set in. I somehow managed to convince him it was unlikely anyone else would be turning up that night.

After a restless night, we woke to a slightly misty but sunny morning. I pretended for the kids' sake that everything was fine as I pottered getting breakfast. Shortly after breakfast the Italian owners turned up and everything was fine. We were in the correct accommodation after all. Colour returned to David's face. We managed to converse with a little Italian and their smattering of English. The setting was breath-taking. We had an amazing view across a deep Tuscan

197

valley and in the daylight, we could see how high up we were. The kids loved the pool despite it being very cold most of the time. My dad ensconced himself on the balcony and made the most of the magnificent view, relaxing, reading and smoking his pipe.

For me, it was the worst holiday I ever had. David did not relax once. He continually attacked, accused and disagreed with me about food, activities, my mood and so on and was extremely unreasonable. He had high anxiety the whole time. Even though my dad was being well-behaved, just his presence meant that David could not relax. He was embarrassingly rude and ridiculous at times. I just wanted to go home.

Despite this, I tried hard to make it a fantastic holiday for the children. The reason we had chosen Tuscany was that the children were keen to see the leaning tower of Pisa, and James was keen to 'eat pizza in Pisa'. The kids love a pun! It was as good a reason as any to go there.

One success of the holiday was our visit to the ancient walled town of Lucca. David and James are quite obsessed with the BBC's *Top Gear* and Lucca had featured heavily in one episode. When I suggested that we visit, everyone agreed. I had done my research and found out that you could hire bicycles and cycle around the famous walls. The day we went, my dad decided to stay behind and rest so it was just the four of us. This probably let David relax a little. Lucca was an hour's drive away but it was worth it. It was truly old and beautiful. We easily found a bike rental place and after handing over a passport as security, were each fitted with a bike. We had a lazy cycle around the town and got to see many of the ancient attractions from the saddle.

The kids enjoyed the physical activity and then we sat al fresco and had coffee and pancakes. It was a good day.

Travelling back from Lucca I texted my dad to say I would pick up a pizza en-route. He replied, saying not to worry but he had locked himself out on the balcony as the wind had blown the door shut. I don't know about you, but when people tell you not to worry I find there is generally something to worry about.

My immediate thought was that if the wind had blown the balcony door shut it must have blown the front door shut too and we had left the keys on the kitchen table for my dad. This hadn't occurred to anyone else. My greatest fear was realised when we arrived. The heavy period door was firmly shut and my dad was still on the balcony with no way of getting out or down. I peered round the side of the house to make sure he was okay. He was looking rather sheepish.

I didn't know how to get hold of the owner as the details were in the kitchen. The villa had a roof terrace and I was pretty sure I hadn't locked the door after using it the night before. I suggested we try and get on to the roof terrace. David and I figured out if we could get a garden bench one of us could scramble on to the tiled roof and clamber up it to the roof terrace. We dragged the bench around to the back of the house where the roof was lowest. I didn't want David to do it as he was too heavy, so I was psyching myself up to climb when James who was eleven at the time, piped up that he would do it. I hadn't considered asking him as I assumed he would be too scared but he was extremely light and it meant we could give him a boost up on to the tiles.

David helped James climb up on to the steeply sloping terracotta tiles and we watched with our hearts in our

199

mouths as James clambered up them. He then managed to climb over the wall of the roof terrace easily. I was praying that I hadn't locked the door to the terrace that morning or we would all be stuck. I couldn't bear the thought of more blame or stress.

Thankfully I needn't have worried and James soon came clattering down the spiral staircase and released his grandfather from his scenic prison. We were so proud of him and my dad was very grateful calling James his hero. I was so pleased that instead of panicking, James had volunteered to help during a crisis.

Encouraged by our successful day in Lucca, we decided to go back and take dad with us. Of course, this time it was a disaster. Dad went flying off his bike within moments of setting off and ended up covered in blood. We carried on but this time it was much busier and there were a lot of people in the way. We stopped for lunch but James got freaked out by wasps and David sweated so much he had sun lotion, that he had plastered on his face, run into his eyes. I had to lead him into the restaurant by his hand as he couldn't see to wash his face. Lord knows what the Italians thought of us!

This holiday certainly seemed to have a problem with heights. Dad came on the day trip to Pisa but decided not to climb the Leaning Tower with us and waited below. The kids however were excited and ran up the steps as fast as the tourists in front would let them. David then refused to go to the top section as I think he thought it was on a slope. It wasn't. I took the kids onto the roof which was very worthwhile to see the rooftops and towers of Pisa.

Of course, the kids got bored before I did and went back down the steep, narrow, worn marble steps before I was ready to join them. I saw them disappear down the narrow staircase and then I saw a large German man bump Cathryn out of the way. I saw her scream and fall and disappear out of sight. I could hear her bumping down the steps and crying. I had visions of her bumping all the way down the spiral staircase to the very bottom of the tower! Thankfully by the time I had caught up she had been taken care of by some lovely Italian attendants who were inspecting her bloodied knees. Cathryn was mortified about her fall and we are not allowed to speak of it – ever.

But I found myself at breaking point the next day. Another falling out with David for no reason other than he was anxious and I hated the fact I was spending the whole of our holiday walking on eggshells, not able to voice an opinion, never knowing what I was going to say next would be hailed as genius or ridiculous.

I had a research assignment due in when I got back to university in September and I was really struggling with the complexities of it. I had used it as an excuse to go and sit quietly outside but the reality was that I was avoiding having to interact with my husband. I was sitting beside the pool in the blazing sunshine with my head in my hands, wondering how I was going to go on but also wondering how I could possibly leave. I was despairing.

The first year of my MA had confirmed to me many times over that my husband was on the autistic spectrum. He didn't need an official diagnosis and indeed he didn't want one. We had learned about children and how early intervention could make such a difference. I had hope for James because of this but I couldn't see any hope for David and I. Was this what the rest of my life was going to be? I must have looked so despairing that even my father who also can't interpret body language, asked me if I was alright.

I have very mixed feelings about the holiday. I think the kids enjoyed themselves but I can't say I did. Italy was beautiful and we have been back several times since but without the addition of extra family members and a more rigid travel plan. I really was considering divorce by the end of the trip.

Things calmed down a little when we got home but one evening David snapped at me about something trivial and I walked away into the kitchen. I felt hurt and broken. The more I dwelt on what my life had become, the less I felt able to deal with it.

I could feel the tears starting to prickle at the backs of my eyes and I started saying to myself, "I can't do this anymore."

David came in to the kitchen wanting to know what the matter was but I had lost control. I just kept crying, "I can't do this anymore. I can't do this anymore."

I vaguely registered the look of fear on David's face. He wanted to know what he could do. He wanted to fix it. He knew tears were bad. I was inconsolable and just kept repeating, "I can't do this anymore."

He promised me lots of things. That he would try harder. He didn't want to lose me. He tiptoed around me for weeks after that until it went back to normal.

The problem with an Asperger marriage is you can't leave because you know you will destroy your partner but you find yourself being broken in the process.

Keeping Secrets

My whole life had become centred around autism and Asperger's. I was completely immersed. Most of my friends either were on the spectrum or had kids on the spectrum. It was pretty much in most of my conversations with whoever I talked to. I would think about it when driving or doing household chores but these were also my best times of quiet contemplation and having quiet revelations about my husband and my kids and how to treat them. I was learning what language to use around them and what triggers to avoid and slowly it was becoming second nature.

In June, I received a letter from the council saying they had received a complaint from a neighbour regarding my dog barking. The letter was scary and threatening. I knew Maddi barked when she was outside but I had never thought it was excessive and none of my immediate neighbours had complained. In fact, the little old lady next door had told me that she never heard her so I hadn't worried about the occasional bout of woofing.

I was truly scared as it turned out they had the power to remove our dog if there was no improvement. I was also upset that the neighbour had not approached me first. I immediately contacted the council but there was no reply. I left a message and then sent a long e-mail asking for clarification.

The hardest thing was not that my neighbour had made a complaint but that I made the decision not to tell David. I told the children that we would have to take great care to stop Maddi barking. When David came home that night he, unusually, asked me how my day had been and what I'd been up to. Any typical husband that could read facial

203

expressions would have immediately seen that something was wrong as I opened and closed my mouth, trying to come up with a reasonable lie. I plumped for

"Nothing much," in the end.

From experience, I knew it was better to keep a secret from David as he would otherwise over react. He would believe that the whole street had got up a campaign against us and would be completely paranoid. Life would be hell.

I had a surprise visit from the man at the council and I invited him in. We had a pleasant chat and I admitted that yes, she did bark but I denied emphatically that she was left alone in the garden all day and other accusations that my neighbour had made. I agreed to keep a diary which apparently, my neighbour was keeping too. Having passed my diary on to the council I heard no more about it. I resolved to tell David after we had moved to a new house.

Update

Oops. David found the letter from the council in a pile of papers on my desk some months after it all happened. He was upset. Not because of what had happened but because I didn't trust him enough to tell him. Despite his upset, it was still a lot less trouble than him finding out at the time. He would not have been able to relax for weeks and would have thought the neighbours were talking about us every time the dog barked. I don't regret not telling him but I do regret my sloppy filing abilities.

Actions Speak Louder than Words

In the winter of 2011, David was working on a community hydro project in North Yorkshire. They were often long days and sometimes he would stay in the little rural village overnight in the local pub. Other days he would drive home very tired and very cold. I discovered one of the reasons for his grumpiness was he was standing in the cold all day long, trying to sort out technical problems with engineers and liaising with local community leaders with no technical ability but lots of enthusiasm. This was mentally exhausting for him. One evening he returned home again after a long day, tired and grumpy. He complained to me how he was still cold after standing in the river for hours on end. I questioned him on this.

"Did someone lend you some wellies?"

"No."

"What were you wearing?" I asked bemused.

"My walking boots." He said, as if it was the obvious answer.

His walking boots were barely more than a pair of trainers and were not waterproof at all. Common sense should dictate that these would be completely ineffectual but it hadn't occurred to him that something could be done about it.

I knew from experience that he hated wearing wellies and that he refused to own a pair, despite my trying to persuade him otherwise. He hardly ever wore a coat and never changed his clothing to suit a situation. I had bought him an expensive waterproof but it rarely saw the light of day. I used to assume that this was his natural northern hardiness

205

but I was beginning to realise that it was more of a sensory problem. He was not aware of his own body temperature unless it was at the extreme end of hot or cold.

I was quite worried about him. I knew that being cold and wet would not stop him from standing in the middle of a river in winter if the job required it. I was determined to get to the bottom of the matter and asked why he didn't like wellies.

"They hurt my calves," he replied.

As a dog walker that lives in the country, I am very familiar with all types of wellies. I had a particularly lovely, expensive pair of neoprene ones that were long, waterproof, thermal and very comfortable. I went off to research short wellies from the same manufacturer.

At Christmas, he opened the large box I gave him with great excitement. His face fell when he saw that inside was just a pair of wellies. They were short and an inoffensive green, made from a tough rubber and neoprene combination with thermal lining. Perfect for standing in shallow rivers for long lengths of time in the winter. I wasn't thanked for my efforts but that didn't bother me.

The next time he went down to Yorkshire to solve a problem, I insisted he put the wellies in the car. He told me he wouldn't use them. He hadn't even tried them on to see if they would fit. He was away a couple of days and the weather had been horrible as only a January in North Yorkshire could be.

David arrived home again after two long days but this time he was in a much more buoyant mood. After he had eaten and relaxed, he remarked to me that he had decided to wear his wellies on the second day as his walking boots were still soaked through from the day before.

He described that not only were they comfortable but his feet stayed warm and dry throughout the day. It enabled him to think and work more efficiently. He was telling me this as if I'd never worn wellies in my life and that he had in fact invented the product himself. You can't convert an Aspie to your own ideas, they must come to their own conclusion and own the idea for themselves. He never directly thanked me for my thoughtful gift. That was all the acknowledgement I got. Yet, I know deep down he was grateful for my thoughtfulness and felt loved by it.

Normal Family Holiday 2.0

We were starting to learn what type of holiday suited our family and had booked our French holiday with care. For a start, it wasn't in Italy. We knew the language, though we didn't know the Pyrenees well but I had been to Carcassonne twice in my youth. Carcassonne is a real fairy-tale castle with towers and many pointed turrets. It is a very touristy town but still worth a revisit. We booked a holiday cottage for a week, a couple of hours drive away from Carcassonne airport.

We partly chose this location as we wanted to go somewhere with a direct flight. As Ryanair is the only airline to fly there and they only fly on a Thursday or a Sunday we had to find accommodation for a few extra days. David booked an apartment hotel room in Nîmes, which was on the way to our villa. We had tried to be as prepared as possible and David had even entered all our destinations into the GPS before we had left home. In theory, all he had to do was plug it into the hire car and off we go.

Our flight arrived without any hitches and we knew we had plenty of time, and more to the point daylight, to get to our first destination. The hire car was not what we had ordered but we decided just to deal with it. We drove to Nimes on a lovely day in 35°C heat. We had time to stop at a Supermarket and stock up on groceries. We arrived in Nîmes with no problems, but as we got nearer to our destination we found that the GPS was trying to send us down one-way streets in the wrong direction. We kept going around and round in circles getting more and more frustrated that we could not find the avenue where the Cheval Blanc hotel was situated. David kept listening to the sat-nav and kept driving around the same streets without stopping. I told him to stop so we could assess the situation but he was getting more and more frustrated and not listening to me at all.

He simply would not stop the car and we must have done the same frustrating circuit about six times, despite the signs remaining the same each time we circuited. His reactions were becoming more hysterical and I was desperately trying to stay calm whilst at the same time persuade him to stop. It was like the information just did not compute and he would only listen to the voice of John Cleese driving us around in circles. The more hysterical he got the less he listened to me. I wanted to try to use the GPS on my 'phone to see if that made any difference. At times like this I do wonder why we go on holiday. Is it social convention? Because it certainly isn't relaxing.

It was becoming a nightmare. Eventually I did manage to persuade him to stop and to use the sat-nav on my new 'phone. This eventually led us down a street that we had not already tried and got us on to the Avenue D'Arenes only to find nowhere to park. I jumped out of the car and talked to the receptionist in my schoolgirl French while she indicated in her halting English that the car park was underground and a short walk away. We drove in the direction she pointed and due to complicated roadworks, ended up driving in the bus lanes. The situation was so ridiculous we all burst out into hysterical laughter as we could not find our way back on to the normal road. Eventually we saw the sign for the well-hidden underground car park and had to trail our luggage about five hundred yards to the hotel.

The air-conditioned room was very welcoming and I collapsed on to the bed just relieved to know we had made

209

it. After a short time, I got up and opened the enormous shutters. We were at the front of the hotel on the Avenue D'Arènes and I could not believe that in my stress I had not noticed we were directly opposite a magnificent Roman Arena, a smaller but complete version of the Coliseum in Rome.

We later found out that overnight, Nîmes City Council had changed all the road signs round so that the locals had woken up to find everything changed and all their cars facing in the wrong direction. Even though we had updated our TomTom the night before there was no way we could have avoided this stress. And that was just the start of our holiday.

On our first full day in Nimes we had to visit the breath-taking Arenes de Nîmes. It was extremely hot inside, walking on the stone benches and having the blazing sunshine reflecting at us from the sand on the Arena floor. David and Cathryn enjoyed listening to the English audio tour guide but James, a budding teenager was much less impressed. That afternoon, we drove to the Pont du Gard, the Roman aqueduct I remember visiting as a child. I remember it being impressive and we were not disappointed. There were a lot of French holiday-makers there enjoying the beautiful weather and leaping off the cliffs in to the river below with little thought for health and safety which had my Aspies on edge.

We hadn't gone prepared for swimming and diving, so we just paddled to cool off. James noticed a number of contented-looking families drifting by in large canoes and to our surprise announced he would like to try canoeing. As it was late afternoon we promised him we would try and do some canoeing later in the week, either nearer our villa or back at that very spot.

We left the hotel in Nîmes the following morning and drove to the tiny hilltop village to our villa. The French owner met us and started speaking rapidly in French. I only managed to catch a few words and when he saw my bewildered look he started laughing and spoke to us in perfect English. It was his little bit of amusement. He knew the odds were that our French would be terrible.

At that point David relaxed and he put on his act of man in charge while we were shown around the owner's home. David's French vocabulary is quite good but he refuses to speak the language unless he must, which means he relies on me and my terrible French to get by. I'm less scared of making mistakes.

David absolutely hated the little car. We had asked for a Renault Scenic but had been given an 'equivalent' an Opal Meriva. I'd never even heard of them. It was the weirdest little car. The kid's doors opened backwards and it was nowhere near the size of a Scenic. We could barely get two bags in the boot and I felt cramped sitting in the passenger seat. It didn't have a proper handbrake and that completely threw David. It was just a little button that you flicked with your finger but he could never tell whether it was on or off. He didn't like it at all. He didn't trust it. The village where we were staying was very picturesque, set on a hill with narrow, winding cobbled streets. The locals drove their little cars like maniacs whizzing up and down these stone alleys without a care for whose right of way it was.

The reckless driving of the locals and the unreliability of the car just made David more and more nervous. The more nervous he got the less control he had over the car. One day after a trip out, we were scuttling up the cobbled street when we had to give way to a young French driver. We were in a very precarious position on a steep cobbled bit of lane and David could not get the handbrake to work. The car kept slipping and slipping back down the cobbles towards an ancient house and ditch. He panicked more and more but eventually got the car to stand still. Moments like that just sucked the enjoyment out of our holiday. In hindsight, I don't think it was the cars fault. I don't think he ever learned to trust the handbrake and wouldn't give it a chance to work.

That car ended up being his nemesis though. We decided we would take the kids to a water park in Marseilles. It was quite a drive away so we left early in the morning to get there. However, it turned out to be the day that the sun did not come out. In fact, thunderstorms were threatening and when we got to the park they were turning people away in droves. It started to pelt it down with rain and we decided to cut our losses and went and found a McDonalds to shelter in. At least we could have hot drinks and make use of their Wi-Fi. We spent an hour in there while I played cards with the kids. Eventually the sun came back out and we decided to go and see a bit more of Marseilles. I was very disappointed with Marseilles as it was quite industrialised and didn't have any of the typical architecture that we liked to see. David very condescendingly pointed out it was a port and not a touristy place. I asked him if he had been there before and he admitted he had once. Not that he had thought to mention it.

Well, regardless of the lack of things to do we decided to have lunch and this involved parking the pesky car. We spotted a sign for parking and had to dive down what looked like a subway in the middle of the road. It was a strange cavernous car park with weird blue lighting. We had to descend quite a few levels before we found a parking space. As we got out of the car David started to panic.

"Where's my 'phone? I've lost my 'phone!"

He was patting all his pockets and searching the various storage compartments in the car. It wasn't there.

"Either I've left it at McDonalds or someone has stolen it!" he announced aggressively.

Now, I was certain he had not left it at McDonalds as I was in 'mum mode' when we left and I distinctly remember checking the table and floor for abandoned and precious items and toys. We hadn't left anything behind.

"I'll ring your 'phone. It's probably just slipped under the seat, or in a bag," I reassuringly tried to tell him.

Of course, we were many levels underground and I didn't have a signal. David got us all back in the car, shouting at the kids and getting more angry and hysterical. He decided I must be wrong and we would have to go back to McDonald's. As we came up the concrete ramp and back into the blinding, noon day sun, I rang David's 'phone. I prayed to God that it would ring. It did, from deep beneath our seats. It was like the sun had broken out on David's face too. We had to stop the car at the side of the busy boulevard to root around under the seat until he eventually found it. By this time, the adrenaline had worn off and I was literally shaking. I was so relieved as I knew how awful the holiday would have been if he hadn't been able to find it. I was mentally exhausted just from those few minutes of having to be the adult and try and keep him calm and

213

pretend to the kids that everything was fine. I must say; the kids tend to switch off from it now. I think if I remain calm then they decide there is nothing to get fussed about. They are used to daddy's moods and know it is best to stay well out of it. I can' blame them for ignoring him and putting their headphones in.

Once David had calmed down, he inspected the console areas of the Meriva in the daylight. He discovered that in the central console, which is supposedly designed to hold wallets, 'phones and other miscellany, there was a perfect sized hole to allow 'phones to slip through and under the seat. We endured that car for the rest of the holiday, but were so happy to hand it back at the end. You can only imagine his reaction the following year, when we arrived at Toulouse airport, having decided to spend twice as much money on a car this year, to be given the keys to another Opel Meriva!

Four Go Canoeing

We were so surprised that James had shown interest in doing a physical activity, that we promised him that we would find out if we could try out canoeing nearer to our villa. The villa did not have internet as promised so we had to make regular daily trips to a McDonalds every day to satisfy David and James' craving to get online. There, I managed to locate, Ceze Canoes. We could hire kayak canoes to travel the Ceze Gorge. It was a twenty-minute drive away and the information in helpful English said it was ideal for beginners. You had to be over the age of 7 and able to swim. It sounded perfect. Excitedly, we used our best French to hire two canoes for an eight kilometre, one way expedition. This was the Rowlands family being intrepid!

We were shown how to stow our belongings into a waterproof barrel that would be carried on one canoe. We took a child each and pushed off. Well, I think the last time I had been in a canoe I was aged ten on a PGL holiday in West Wales. I hadn't remembered anything I had been taught. Annoyingly, I found it hard to steer and kept crashing into the bank and getting stuck in foliage and bending tree branches. David on the other hand, who surprisingly had done a fair amount of sailing on Kielder Reservoir as a teenager, was disappearing off into the distance. He didn't look back. I had to scream at him for help. This was an ominous start.

It helped my pride a little to see that I wasn't the only one struggling. There were two other British tourists having an unhappy time, facing the wrong direction on the flowing river too. They soon gave up and turned back.

David eventually noticed we weren't behind him and James and came back and rather short-temperedly issued instructions to me and Cathryn. We managed to get the hang of it and for a short while all was well. I told myself I could do this. It didn't last long. Due to the excellent weather, there was a shortage of water in places to negotiate shallow rapids and waterfalls. We had to keep getting out of the boat to drag it over the rocks. It was horribly slippery and although shallow, the water was still quite forceful. I slipped and fell repeatedly, grazing my hands and knees. At one point, I was steering the boat over a shallow, fast flowing rapid, when the current whisked the boat containing my daughter, away from my guiding hands and off down the Ceze. I had to shriek at David ahead of me, to grab our little girl as she flew by.

It was slow, painful progress. I started to hate every minute. We noticed other tanned European families whisking past us merrily while we were soaked through. I wondered when this nightmare was going to end.

Tired, we had a short break and then swapped children. By this time, I was worried we were lagging behind time and would miss the bus that was scheduled to pick us up at the rendezvous point. We had no concept of how far we'd come as there were no markers, where we were going to or how long it would take us to get there. The children were getting tired, as were David and I but I had to pretend to be calm and cheerful and chivvy them along.

After a while we entered a calm open expanse of river, almost like a lake and James and I got into a rhythm. I started to let myself enjoy the beautiful scenery. When I looked back to see whether David and Cathryn were enjoying themselves too, they were nowhere to be seen. Literally nowhere!

The last bend was about half a mile away. Where were they? Had they given up? Capsized and drowned? I had to make James stop paddling and help me look for them. This was really turning into a nightmare! I was just starting to wonder if I could get reception on my mobile and ring French emergency services when we suddenly saw them appear through the trees from the furthest bend. I was so relieved. As I got closer I saw that they were soaked through and Cathryn was crying. David looked very pale and somewhat traumatised.

At the last resting place, they had tried to get back into their canoe but it constantly kept capsizing. It may well have been their mismatched weight that made it worse. I was so relieved to see them both but I was shaky from terror and tiredness. I literally didn't know if we could continue. I could see David looked desperately grim, but I could also tell he wasn't ready to give up. He wanted this over as much as I did and we knew we just had to keep going. So, we kept on keeping on, with whimpering children and us pretending all was fine. We still didn't see the sign for the finish and getting the bus. We had been canoeing for hours!

Up ahead on the bank, I saw some signs of life and told David I was stopping to ask for directions or help. We decided we needed another rest anyway. I staggered up the pebbly bank, drenched and muddy and saw I was at an activity centre. A lady came towards me and asked me enquiringly in French what I wanted. I did my best to reply. Once she realised I was English she answered me in her Yorkshire accent. To my delight, she knew exactly where we were headed and told me it was literally just another ten minutes canoeing down the river and on the left-hand side. We couldn't miss it. I wanted to hug her and thanked her profusely. God knows what she thought of this bedraggled wretch in front of her.

My news was met with great excitement and invigoration and we all found our energy again. Thankfully, it was exactly as the young Yorkshire lass had described and we eventually found the spot to disembark, pour the water out of our canoes and shoes and wait for the bus. We were at least an hour late but we hoped there would be another one along soon. Gradually, more canoeists started to appear and arrive at the gravel bank. Some looked just as shattered and stressed as we were, whilst others were happily chatting away to each other.

On the way home, we stopped off at the nearest supermarket to stock up on chocolate and wine. Both are good for shock! I had a very long, hot bath when I got in and it took a long time for warmth to arrive and tension to leave my limbs. We have all vowed never to go canoeing again!

James said that if he ever came up with a good idea like that again that we should shoot him.

Dark Times

To my delight in September 2012 I discovered I had passed the second year of my Masters and was now contemplating the third and most exciting year where I would be concentrating on my dissertation.

With excitement, I met the two Helens from my course with whom I was good friends. They had also passed and we went along to a dissertation event where we could talk to all the lecturers who were looking to be our supervisors.

I had already given my course tutor an outline of what I wanted to do. I knew it was controversial and hadn't been done before. I had searched the internet and the university database to find a research paper on autism and adult relationships.

Both my course tutor and research methods tutor had approved my proposal but they could not supervise me. I was introduced to academic staff whose specialisms were autism or disability. At first, they seemed intrigued by what I was proposing but as we got further into discussion about how personal the subject was, I realised they looked concerned and were backing off. This wasn't like anything they had come across before and they didn't want to risk getting involved.

As the weeks went by, my fellow students had arranged their mentors for the year but I alone hadn't. It was very disheartening. Despite this, I attended different seminars to determine what method I should consider. The academic supervisor advised that I should look into a little known and used type of methodology. It was called autoethnography. This was basically, write my autobiography and do some research on the subject. This sounded perfect to me. The rest of my fellow students were mostly doing analyses or meta-analyses as they didn't have time to do a huge amount of research. I asked whether eighteen years in an autistic relationship was enough and they agreed it was!

Discussing dilemmas with some fellow students during a seminar, I discovered one lady, progressing with her doctorate, was also using the method of autoethnography in disability. She offered to be my supervisor and gratefully I arranged to meet up with her.

I was apprehensive about the meeting with my new mentor, Dawn. In the end, it went better than I'd anticipated. I knew I needed direction and after some gentle questioning, Dawn suggested I needed to write a book about my time with David, if not my life as a child too. She was also keen for me to consider a doctorate in the future. My head swam at the idea!

Self-Doubt

We don't go to the cinema much, but it isn't because David doesn't like to. It is just that he won't go and see just anything. It must be a film of significance and quality. In October 2012, it was the long-awaited James Bond movie, *Skyfall*. The moment the release date was announced I bought the tickets and made sure David kept the date clear in his diary. He waited with great anticipation.

On the day, we dropped our daughter off at her grandmothers for her weekly visit. By the time we were on our way, David was in a foul mood, convinced we were going to be late. I am a punctual person and also hate being late, but I knew we still had time to get there. Besides, everyone knows that the official film listing time is a good half an hour before the film starts. This did not stop David from getting wound-up before we arrived. He enjoyed the film immensely and came out in a better mood. Then he switched his 'phone back on.

He noticed he had a missed call from HMRC. It completely changed his mood and when I mistakenly chatted to him about the possibility of doing a doctorate, he told me it was a waste of time and money. How to put me down!

It made me wonder if he thought what I was studying was a complete waste of time. It was so gutting. He made me feel worthless and pointless. I couldn't hide my resentment.

Raining on our Parade

Later that month, Charlotte and I were asked by the conductor if we would consider singing a soprano solo together. It was a small part in the *Bach Christmas Oratorio* and all the soprano lines were very high. We were both worried that we might not do the part of the angel justice. Jokingly, I suggested to Charlotte that Cathryn should do it but she surprised me by wondering if Cathryn really could.

At home, I asked Cathryn if she would like to sing the part and warned her it would be in front of a large audience. To my surprise, Cathryn leapt at the chance. I said I would have a word with the conductor. The lead Alto, a singing teacher, volunteered to go through the part with Cathryn who was thrilled when she found out she would be having a 'proper' singing lesson.

We went along to Martha's house and Cathryn, though she made a few mistakes, proved that she could sing well. It was agreed that Cathryn should come to our choral practice early to audition for the conductor.

I asked David if he would bring Cathryn home after so I wouldn't miss any practice. He drove us there and found a parking space right outside the door. I asked him if he was coming in but he said he would sit in the car, in case he had to move it. Cathryn nervously but perfectly sang her part for the conductor. He was pleased and I was very proud. I escorted Cathryn back to the car and told David she had passed her audition. He didn't say much so I just said that I'd see him later.

We had a good session and Charlotte and I practised a lovely duet for the concert. I got home on a high, both pleased with myself and my daughter. When I saw David, I asked if he'd spoken to Cathryn about it. He briefly replied he had. I said gently to him, "You could have come in you know," thinking that he had missed out on seeing her audition.

What he said next floored me. He announced that he hadn't come in because he didn't want everyone to think we were 'pushy parents'. All my euphoria dissipated in that moment. He just crushed Cathryn's achievement in a dismissive and negative way. All he could see was that I had suggested her for the part and therefore that was wrong.

I probably hadn't spelled out to him how relieved Charlotte were when we were off the hook. I hadn't forced the situation with the conductor at all, if anyone had cast any doubt, I would have let it go. David has never been part of the choir and doesn't come to church and isn't as involved in the community as I am. Our village has seen Cathryn grow up amongst them, prayed for her when she was ill and seen her baptised and take part in many village activities. He didn't realise how proud and supportive they are of local children and how in fact, taking part is greatly encouraged. Yet in one sentence he filled me with self-doubt.

I didn't argue with him as I knew he had had a terrible and stressful day at work. He had managed to tell me the highlights about what had gone wrong over the weekend with a large engineering project and all the repercussions.

This had set off his paranoia. When he was sitting in the car, he was convinced he had no right to be there. He felt he was occupying space meant for choir members who were arriving and struggling for places to park. He convinced himself they were complaining about him. He says they were all muttering about him. Muttering being the operative word. He couldn't hear what they were saying and they were more likely complaining about the weather.

Catastrophizing

The next film we saw was the long-awaited release of *The Hobbit*. I have been a fan of JRR Tolkien all my life, as our mum used to read *The Lord of The Rings* to my brothers and me when we were little. This time, to avoid David's mood I made sure we left in plenty of time and we wouldn't have to rush to get his favourite cheesy nachos and drinks. He was perfectly happy. We both loved the film despite it being three-hours long, could not believe when it ended. I wanted to stay and see it again.

Okay, that's the good bit. Three hours of fantasy, not thinking about our real world. The moment we came out of the cinema, David started behaving in an agitated manner. We needed money to pay the lovely (rather handsome) handyman we'd hired to fix the tiles in the en-suite and other odd jobs around the house. David however, would not queue up at the cash-machine right next to the cinema. This may be because I said I wasn't hungry enough for lunch as we had eaten in the cinema and that probably threw him. I hadn't stuck to the plan.

Since we had agreed that as a Christmas present he should buy himself a Samsung Galaxy Tablet, (as he liked the one we had already bought for his mother for Christmas) I suggested we go to Tesco and get that and take out the money. However, he started panicking saying we couldn't afford to buy one for him as we had to pay Ash, even though this was money we had accounted for. He vastly overestimated the hours Ash had worked for us and I also had to keep reminding him that I had already paid Ash half the money already.

Silence was held until we got to Tesco when he jumped out of the car and went to withdraw cash. When he came back he was practically in tears, saying that we had no money left in either our joint or business accounts. He couldn't understand where all the money had gone. Neither could I as I had checked out balance the day before and it was more than healthy. I hadn't spent that much!

He was hyperventilating and panicking about how we were going to afford to pay for anything this month and that he hadn't paid the mortgage yet. I could feel my stress levels rising along with my heart rate. I started to think it must be all my fault; that I was spending too much on Christmas.

David refused to get out of the car when we got to his mother's which is always a sign he is in a terrible mood. I kept the chat short, though I did hint at David's mood.

As we drove through the villages on the way home, David slowed the car right down as he saw a police car appear behind him. He became completely paranoid, convinced that the car had targeted him for doing something wrong. He was utterly irrational about being pulled over. There was nothing I could say, as any reassurance from me now would be ignored and I'd probably just get shouted at anyway. I found myself digging my finger nails into my arm. Even after the police car turned off, David was driving extra carefully for some time. His driving was affected, his gear changing was jerky and his speeds on the road were erratic.

Cathryn was in the back of the car reading Harry Potter for the umpteenth time. I don't know whether she realised what was going on. She certainly didn't say anything and I was trying to keep our joint anxiety as low-key as possible.

When we got home, David was momentarily distracted by the arrival of a Christmas parcel that we thought had been lost. Also, James who had been left to fend for himself had not had lunch. I'd left him a step-by-step guide on how to 'cook' noodles. He had raided the fridge instead. David fixated on this and managed to give James the impression that we were cross with him. Poor James was terrified of his dad's stern looks and started whimpering. I assured James that everything was fine and gently admonished David for being so harsh on James.

David's next task was to log on to our online banking systems. With a cry of relief, he saw that we still had plenty of money in our joint account. The business account was also fine. In his self-induced panic, he had not registered the vital digits at all.

Within moments his relief was evident as he started cracking jokes and smiling and laughing. He couldn't understand why I was not reciprocating. I am his emotional sponge and I take a while to be wrung out and bounce back.

Counselling

In February, my mood was very low. The weather was awful; the days were so dark. I was getting little sleep due to David's terrible snoring, and I just felt dejected, fed-up, unmotivated and daunted by the thought of this marriage continuing like that for evermore. I started to wonder if I was depressed. I made an appointment with the GP but had to wait over a week to speak with him. I suppose subconsciously I was hoping for him to wave a magic wand and make everything better.

After some discussion, the GP decided I wasn't depressed but under a lot of pressure and stress. He thought counselling would help but warned me there was a waiting list. My appointment arrived a few weeks later. It was for 11th June!

In March, David was seeing the same GP about his psoriasis and on his next visit, they agreed that his skin was improving a little. The doctor was more interested in doing something about David's weight. I liked the fact that the doctor had informed him that it was his responsibility and not mine to deal with this. He recommended David see a dietician and have his bloods tested.

We went back to reception and David told the receptionist that he needed to make an appointment for a fasting blood test. The woman behind the desk offered him the next Wednesday. David said he would check his diary and got his 'phone out. He spent an inordinate amount of time staring fixedly at the screen to the point where it was getting uncomfortable. I didn't say anything as I didn't want to pressure him. Aspies live in a different time zone and need more processing time than the rest of us. Unfortunately, the

227

receptionist, not used to my husband, tried to be helpful by offering him another date. David impatiently snapped,

"If you could just wait! I'm trying to see if that Wednesday is okay!"

David then got extremely flustered and stomped off back to the car, leaving me standing there. I called after him but he ignored me. I turned back to the receptionist and said,

"I'll make the appointment."

She didn't bat an eye and just asked me what he was like fasting.

"A bit like that, really," I said, grimacing.

I made the original appointment with her and said I would change it if it was no good. I nearly told her about his Asperger's but what was the point? I found David waiting outside in the car and gently said that I had made him the Wednesday appointment. He seemed okay with me taking control of that.

Yet, all the way home he raged about how rude and controlling the receptionist had been and how people were behind us in the queue harrumphing. I tried to explain that she was just doing her job and trying to be helpful. In his eyes, she was 'trying to control my diary' and 'only I control my diary. It is the thing that pays the mortgage!'.

I gave up defending the poor receptionist in the end as it wasn't going to get me anywhere. I let David rant some more but didn't say anything else. By the time we got home he was convinced he was in my bad books. I assured him he wasn't but I don't think he believed me. However, the best way to overcome this is to change the subject which I did.

Actively not Listening

In June, I nervously went along to what I thought was my first counselling session. Judy introduced herself to me and said this was an assessment session to see whether counselling would be appropriate. I spent ten minutes filling in a questionnaire about my mood.

In the subsequent months since David had visited the GP, we had both started to lose weight. David had been told he was borderline diabetic. Hearing this from an expert had scared him into action and he lost two stone in weight. The healthier diet and exercise regime had the benefit of improving his snoring. The sun had come out and I had managed to get some sleep. I'm so much happier and resilient when I have adequate sleep.

So, by the time I got to see this counsellor, I didn't know whether I was a candidate or not. It turned out I wasn't. I don't have suicidal thoughts and I like to be sociable with people. My lack of domestic ability scored me a few points but not enough. We did discuss my situation which she found intriguing and suggested that perhaps we needed couples counselling. I told her it wouldn't work for David. He would go if I asked him to but he would hate every minute of it, especially if it was led by someone who was not an ASD specialist.

In the end, she said the only course she could recommend was stress therapy and apart from that, I seemed to be doing well by myself. I went home disappointed, feeling that I'd wasted my time.

On reflection, I had found this treatment and dismissal of my situation appalling. Why would I want to see a counsellor if I was coping? I spent time trying to find a specialist counsellor in the area. There were none. In fact, I only found two in the whole country and one charged £300 for an appointment. It just wasn't accessible at all. I used this information in my dissertation and it started me wondering what one had to do to become a specialist ASD relationship counsellor.

Testing my Sanity

It was the school summer holidays and I was working hard to finish my dissertation. It was due in at the beginning of September. I felt guilty about not paying the kids very much attention, but they were at an age now where they were quite self-sufficient if I kept putting food in the fridge and the Wi-Fi was working. My intention was to get my dissertation mostly finished and then enjoy a ten-day holiday in France where I wouldn't have to think about it at all. I would then have a couple of weeks when the children were back at school where I could devote full concentration and finish my dissertation off.

One day, David made several comments about my course which genuinely made me doubt myself and what I was doing. The first was, surely, I had finished by now as he had calculated that it should only take me twenty hours to complete it. Where he had plucked this number from I have no idea. The second comment was that he didn't consider my Masters to be a postgraduate course. In one fell swoop, he had just told me what I was doing was a waste of time and that I wasn't even very good at that. Normally, I would let comments like this go by, but I stood up for myself and told him that of course I was studying for a postgraduate qualification. Some days he is so supportive of me and the next he is cruel and condescending and I have no idea why. He says it all with such conviction that I start doubting myself. Was I actually doing a Masters level course?

His next trick was to help me further with my dissertation. He had already pointed out that I was taking too long on it. In my head, I had always had a year. A year to plan, write the autoethnography, apply to ethics, reapply to ethics, interview my subjects, transcribe and analyse the data and finally write it up. I was in the writing up stage. All my interviews with fellow Asperger wives had been conducted months before and I had transcribed the audio and converted it into qualitative data. Now I was looking at correlations between my life and theirs. I was coming up with insights and solutions supported with academic references. This all took time, especially as at the same time I was a full-time mum and wife. Yet, for the last month, I had stopped having a social life, something he considered frivolous anyway, and concentrated fully on my work and the impending deadline.

I think it was his way of letting me know that I wasn't giving him enough attention; but I wasn't giving anything in my life attention other than my work and we all knew it would soon be at an end.

I had several chapters open on my desktop; open or minimised, depending on what I was working on or what I would suddenly get inspired to write about. I knew where everything was and what I was doing with it. We worked in the same study. It was quiet except when he was on the 'phone to clients. He never considered whether I needed space to think, though he always disapproved greatly of anyone else making any noise when he was working.

I came to a natural pause and decided to take pity on the dog whose walks were few and far between at that time. David had shown more curiosity about my progress so I said he could read it my research so far, if he wished.

I needed a break. The weather was lovely and I had made so much progress and needed to get away from my desk so the dog and I had a substantial walk. When I got back however,

David was sitting happily at this desk with his arms folded and a self-satisfied smirk on his face.

"I've sorted it out for you," he told me proudly.

"Sorted what out?" I asked apprehensively.

"Your dissertation," he remarked in patronising tones.

"What do you mean?" I dreaded the answer.

He proceeded to tell me how he had put all my chapters together into one document; added the contents page and automated it so any updates would change automatically. He had stylised all the separate title headings and sub-paragraphs to his liking and convenience.

I want to say I couldn't believe what he had just done to my work but unfortunately, I did believe it. When he saw how upset I was at this desecration, he got angry with me for not appreciating all *his* hard work on *my* behalf. I was an ungrateful wife.

What it came down to, was that he knew this was very important to me and he couldn't cope with not being in control of it. He didn't trust me to do a good job. He twisted it in his head that he was helping me. In fact, all he succeeded in doing was making me angry, upset and violated. He had slowed me down. I'd known exactly where everything had been and where to find it and now my thousands of words were lumped together in one extremely long document I had to scroll through constantly. It was time-consuming and frustrating and somehow, I was the bad person for not appreciating this!

I remember joking that it would be ironic if this dissertation about our marriage was the end of our marriage but it very nearly came close to it.

The sad thing is, that a lot of what he did for me was very good work but I hated every bit of it because it wasn't mine. If he had offered to help me set out my document in a stylised way, I would have gratefully accepted. He would have got credit for it. Instead, his controlling nature ruined it for both of us.

Somehow, I managed to calm down and get through my masters degree. I had to. This deadline was too important to me.

Status Symbol

Our new car was due to arrive a couple of days after my dissertation was due in and David was really looking forward to receiving it. He had never had an Audi before and it was a status symbol he felt he deserved for all his hard work. I was pleased for him but my mind was on other things. A week before it was due to arrive, the garage rang up with 'good' news. The car had arrived early! Well, it wasn't good news to me. I wanted to get my dissertation out of the way before accepting the car, but it was too late.

He arranged for the handover to happen the next day. The kids were excited, so we decided that we would all drive down, pick up the car and I would drive back in the 'old' car. It became a bit of an outing as we decided to grab lunch at a nearby farm restaurant while we were there. The handover took a long time and I stood outside with the kids for ages, waiting patiently. Eventually, everyone was satisfied. The Audi garage tried to hand over a bouquet of flowers to me which I declined. What a ridiculous thing and a waste of money. The man gets the car and the little woman gets the flowers? Not interested.

I followed David out of the car park but it took for ever for the lights to change and he stalled the Audi. We had to wait for the lights to change again before we could leave the forecourt. The restaurant was literally a couple of hundred yards down the road so we both drove there and parked up. The moment he got out of the car I could tell something was wrong but I didn't mention it. He was distant during lunch and then I tailed him home. He drove very slowly. I stopped following him after a while, refusing to travel in such a slow convoy and got home first with Cathryn. James was in the car with David.

By the time they arrived back, David had decided he hated the car. He wasn't going to drive it. Ever again! He told me I would have to drive it. He would drive the other car.

I didn't have time for this kind of ridiculous meltdown. I had just a few days to fine-tune my work. David was focussing everything onto himself. I called his bluff. I told him that fine, I would drive it.

I took James to school in the new car the following morning. David decided to come for the ride. Just what I needed!

The first time I had driven it with its new-fangled hand brake and fancy electronic equipment and he wanted to watch and judge. He spent the whole time either criticising my driving or telling me what a wonderful car it was and what all the fancy gadgets did. He was making me nervous and I hadn't got the hang of the little switch which was the handbrake and the traffic was heavy. I was getting stressed and he got more stressed because of it.

Somehow, I got James to school without any mishap but it wasn't a great start to my day when I needed to be calm and concentrate. His lack of empathy for my situation was astonishing.

Miraculously, I managed to finish my dissertation a whole day early. David, and I will give him credit here, helped me check every detail and reference. His pedantry and eye for detail really came in handy.

The next day, I needed to get my work printed and bound before delivering it to the university. David was very tired having spent half the night checking my references. I told him I didn't want to drive the Audi as I was too nervous about handing my work in. Instead, I suggested he could drive and we would take the old car into town.

The most bizarre thing happened. Once the ink was dry on my three unbound copies, he suddenly relaxed. He decided he *would* drive the new car after all. He wanted to give it another chance. I wasn't happy about this but said nothing. I didn't want his mood to wreck my day as I needed to make sure I got the copies bound in time.

To my great relief, everything went off without a hitch. The copies went in for binding. We had a nice lunch, picked up the bound copies and delivered to the accepting office. I was a relieved, exhausted mess. My husband; he was on a high!

He decided not only did he like his new car but that we would go home via the scenic route. This meant that we drove through the countryside at lightning speed, whipping around bends and overtaking other slower moving cars. Now he felt relaxed and able to drive his dream car the way he had always wanted to. I on the other hand hung onto the seat and closed my eyes waiting to crash, annoyed that I had done all that work for nothing. We were surely going to die!

Epilogue: 2016

I wrote the above memoirs as part of my dissertation in 2013, never with the intention of sharing them with the world other than my supervisors, Dawn Benson and David Littlefair.

I was almost in tears reading back through some of my notes and in fact, the worst bit to read was how accepting I was at the time that this is the best that my marriage would get. I wasn't defeatist, just being pragmatic but it was so sad. It was almost like reading another person's memoirs rather than my own.

So, where are we now, and what has happened since then?

Something seemed to click with David after reading my dissertation. He realised that it wasn't all about him. He came to see over a period of time, that his behaviour affected me; that it had profound consequences. I believe that reading my dissertation and having my thoughts and feelings validated by other women, brought home to him that I wasn't being over sensitive. It made him review his own behaviour. He didn't want me to be unhappy. He could see how much I was trying in our relationship and realised he had to pull his weight too.

This was a big step and only he could come to this conclusion. The thought process had to be his own and the decision to change had to be his own. You can lead an Aspie to water but you can't make them drink.

Better still, I received a First for all my hard work. He couldn't not be proud of me for that, especially after all his input!

238

By achieving such a high mark, it proved to him that thoughts and words he considered as just fluff, had been validated by experts. This started to make him see that I knew what I was talking about. That he should start listening to me a bit more. Previously, he had just seen me as an enthusiastic amateur, dabbling in the area of autism.

This is a trait I have noticed and written about previously in our first book; *Asperger Marriage and Relationships: Insight from the Front Line*, that our partners will only act on the Voice of Authority and not because we have told them something.

Indeed, I have friends on the spectrum who have known me a long time, who even though they now know I am qualified in this area, cannot look past friendship mode and take on board I am now an expert in this field. It's very hard to move from the friendship zone into the Voice of Authority zone. You really do have to prove yourself.

Improving our Health and our Relationship

One of the physical signs of stress in David was his psoriasis. It started off by little patches on his arms and then he started getting areas on his chest and back. These patches were getting larger and redder. He would constantly pick at them. They looked unhealthy and uncomfortable. He had never been to the doctor about his psoriasis and didn't seem inclined to do anything about it either. I tried to get him to use certain lotions after being in the shower or use a special medicated shampoo. They didn't work but mainly because he never used them. He didn't believe they would work. Well, that was self-perpetuating!

As his stress levels increased, so the patches started to spread and I noticed it was creeping down his scalp, into his hairline and onto his face. It was also getting so bad it was bleeding through the back of his shirt. He still wouldn't do anything about it. He knew it was stress related and seemed to think it was just something he had to put up with.

I started doing some research online and came across a lot of information that suggested that psoriasis was caused, not just by stress but by vitamin D deficiency. David is hardly a sun worshipper so it seemed probable he did have a deficiency. I managed to persuade him to take one pill a day. He was reluctant at first, but I also read taking it with orange juice helped its effectiveness. I would hand him a glass of orange juice, then stand over him until he took the pill. It soon became a routine and he realised his life would be easier if he just did this one simple thing I asked of him every day.

Slowly, after several weeks, with my persistence, I started to see a small change in the quality of David's skin. After a couple of months even he couldn't deny that his skin was improving. Yet, something subtler, imperceptible at first, was that his moods had not been as up and down as usual. I wondered if it was just coincidence, or whether taking vitamin D had anything to do with the slight improvement in his behaviour.

After an extensive search on Google Scholar I came across an interesting paper where research had been carried out with families of autistic children and taking controlled Vitamin D supplements. The instructions to the parents was to give their children three drops of vitamin D3 a day in the child's juice, for several weeks. When reporting back to the researchers, most parents had not noticed any significant improvement in their child's behaviour but a few had noticed their children become calmer, happier and were sleeping better. On further questioning, the researchers discovered that the children who had shown significant improvement were the ones whose parents had misread the instructions! They had been dosing their children with three *pipettes* of vitamin D3 a day and not the three drops as prescribed! The children had come to no harm through the 'overdosing' and in fact had benefitted greatly from it.

I was intrigued to have my own thoughts confirmed. I started to investigate further and considered dosing David with higher amounts of vitamin D3. What levels were safe? I found a significant difference in opinion wherever I looked. A lot of it was helpful though.

I doubled David's dose. I also started to add magnesium to his selection of pills in the morning and read a book by a self-published author who had experimented on himself with extremely high doses of vitamin D3. This person mentioned that it was possible to overdose if you took incredibly high doses. He was taking 100,000 international units (iu) a day! That was twenty-five times the strength I was giving David. He reported that after doing this for a while, he began to ache but then discovered that if you introduce vitamin K2 into the mix just once a week, that this helps the body distribute the Vitamin D3 to the correct places. The aching stops and the body can work on renewing plentiful cells, drastically reducing the risk of cancer, lethargy, gut problems, multiple sclerosis, the list is almost endless.

I'm not advocating taking such high doses as I don't believe there is any need to do this unless you are suffering from a disease such as multiple sclerosis. I understand there is a new and innovate regime called the Coimbra Protocol which is advocates controlled high doses of vitamin D3 to reverse mild and severe MS.

It took me many months to discover, sort through, read and evaluate all this information but it was worth it.

See the benefits, I joined David every morning by supplementing with a growing number of vitamins which now included 6000 iu of vitamin D3, a capsule of Omega 3, 400 mg of magnesium, vitamin B complex. Both the magnesium and vitamin B help with anxiety and which I discovered our modern diet is deficient in due to intensive farming. Not forgetting the weekly and vital dose of K2.

Furthermore, I learned how new research is discovering that a healthy gut lead to a healthy mind and brain. David and I probably both suffered from leaky gut syndrome. It made sense to me because of my long-term wheat and lactose intolerance and I already knew what a difference it had made to my life, eliminating wheat and dairy from my diet.

We had come a long way in just a few months but David was not prepared to change his diet for me or his health. He was overweight and I was not attracted to him anymore. He was prepared to take the pills for me as that was easy, but he was not prepared to give up his favourite comfort foods for anyone.

Transformation

Our relationship, overall, was gradually improving. We were much happier and more tolerant of each other. Reduced anxiety and more patience lead to better communication.

Our daughter was in the long process of getting a formal diagnosis, also of ASD or Asperger's Syndrome. We had all known for a while that she was on the spectrum, but so-called professionals kept putting obstacles in our way. We had at last managed to get an assessment for her and David came along to give his perspective. It obviously got him thinking about his behaviour and how it affects others. After the consultation, he turned to me and advised,

"I'm giving you advance notice that I am going to be horrible this weekend."

I looked at him curiously until he elaborated,

"I have my tax returns to do and I hate doing them."

This was a major step for David. He recognised that he was getting anxious about doing a job he hated. He predicted how this anxiety was going to make him feel and then a further thought process considered how his subsequent behaviour would affect me.

This was so good to hear! It had never happened before. He may have previously had thoughts along these lines before but he was never able to verbalise them. I was touched that he thought of me, but I was also pleased for him. It meant he trusted me enough to be honest and show his weaknesses to me. Thank goodness, I answered him sympathetically.

The ironic twist is that that weekend, though he wasn't in the best of moods, because he had anticipated how bad it could be – and believe me his irritable, condescending behaviour to me at these times can be quite extreme – it just didn't happen.

243

I was careful around him; offered him coffee when he needed it but kept out of the way otherwise. He was less tense and didn't have to worry about the social responsibilities he thinks are required of him over a weekend. Instead, he could fully concentrate on his task and get it done quicker and with less mishap than usual.

What a breakthrough!

So how did this change in attitude come about? Well, that's not a straight forward question to answer but I have given hints and clues along the way. You will have to read our book *Asperger Marriage and Relationships: Insights from the Front Line* for the nitty gritty explanations and his point of view.

But basically, it is a combination of the following:

Love and Understanding

Let him know you love him. Tell him regularly. Don't wait for him to tell you. This is often a case of double standards as they feel that once they have told you, they don't have to tell you again. However, if you don't tell them regularly you are just compounding their feelings of low self-worth.

Patience

It's hard I know but remind yourself he truly does think differently from you. It is easier to think of his problems as a disability at times like this. If his disability was visible you would be more patient with him. Count to ten or walk away. The less combative you become the more he will respond well to you.

Communication

Tell him exactly what you mean. Don't issue complex instructions. Do make your instructions clear. He is most likely a visual thinker so write lists, use a white board. Don't overwhelm him with too much.

Knowing what the Triggers are

This is where you need to be an emotional detective. You will already know what a lot of his triggers are. Does he hate shopping? If he has go to, make sure it's when it's quiet or frequent smaller stores which can be less overwhelming. If he behaves in an irritable way during an expedition, try and find out later what it was that upset him. Look upon it as teamwork. A detective game. What are the challenges and how can we improve them?

Giving each other Space

Letting him have his down time. Let him go into his man cave and play games or sit quietly on his 'phone. He needs this time to recharge and it is not a personal attack on you. By both acknowledging and putting aside time for him to do this he can then relax fully without feeling guilty he should be doing something else. Not being able to have time to 'not think' can lead to explosive meltdowns or a long-term shutdown.

Learning to admit when wrong

We all get things wrong from time to time. We are all proud and don't like to back down. He hates to admit he is wrong. However, admitting to your partner when *you* are wrong leads to defusing arguments and forgiveness. This is true for both neurotypical and autistic partners. However, the autistic partner is much less likely to ever admit that they were wrong. If on the other hand you lead by example, this may, one day happen.

Picking your Battles

Before you begin an argument, consider whether it is really worth it. What would happen if you just let it go? Be the bigger person and walk away. This means when you do stand up for something they are much more likely to take notice.

Supplementation of Diet with Vitamins

An Asperger diet can be very restricted. Some may be health fanatics but many are not as they will only eat certain types of food. Also, many Aspies prefer to stay indoors than go outside and will be deficient in natural Vitamin D.

Reducing Wheat and Dairy Products in Diet

Not long after this major step in our relationship, I came across a book called *Feed Your Brain: Lose Your Belly* by Larry McCleary. I read this avidly. I was keen to see what else I could do for David and thought it might be a bonus if he could lose a little weight too.

It was very complex and went deep into the science of why we put on weight in modern society, the cause of diabetes and how many foods affect the way we think. Basically, I learned that a low carbohydrate diet is highly recommended. At first it seemed extreme to me. I had known friends who had followed the Atkins Diet years before and who had lost a lot of weight but they all had put it back on again

This particular author, doctor and scientist also highly recommended the use of coconut oil. I had already read how good this was potentially for health so I decided to introduce myself slowly to a low carb diet and to start using coconut oil for cooking where I could.

Quietly, I reduced my carbohydrate intake. This meant cutting out all sugar, grains and certain fruits. I was determined to see if it would work and I quickly started to lose weight. It's always lovely the first time someone notices. I also found I had much more energy and I took up running a mile every other morning. I'd never felt so good. David started to notice and was very complimentary about my shape but he showed no interest in joining me.

I knew from experience it wasn't worth nagging and pushing him on this subject. I continued with my own diet and fitness regime. One day, David decided to join me. He refused to read up on the subject (I presume that would be giving in) but he did ask me a few questions and surprised himself by realising that what I had said about eating low carb was not as difficult as he imagined. He did not feel hungry eating protein and fat instead of wheat and sugar filled processed foods.

It has been much more enjoyable to eat this way together. At one point, I would find myself cooking three different meals a night as the children never eat with us.

Now David has lost five stone! I am so proud of him and think he looks more attractive now. What is most obvious though is how happier and healthier he looks. He no longer huffs and puffs when walking upstairs or carrying things. He has stopped complaining so much about everything. He genuinely feels happier and heathier in body and mind. Our summer holiday was much more enjoyable this year as he didn't get too hot, was able to wear shorts, walk up hills and even suggested climbing tall towers in the heat.

Now here is my disclaimer:

This is not a miracle cure. What has happened is that I have now got back the man I married. The one that couldn't do enough for me and was always cheerful and enthusiastic. We have not cured his autism or Asperger's. Even if there was a cure we wouldn't want it. What this has done is created the best Asperger husband there could possibly be.

Improvements	Stayed the Same
• Mood	• Still never makes me a cup of coffee
• Health	• Forgets to pass on vital messages
• Sleep	• Worries what people will think of him
• Feeling of being loved and wanted	• Needs constant esteem boost
• Companionship	• Needs his space
• Teamwork	• Wants me around
• Rationality	• Can't read facial expressions
• Empathy	• Worries overly
• Paranoia	• Reliability
• Motivation	• Lack of identity and self-awareness

We are genuinely so much happier. We are now sharing a room again, after having slept separately for two years, mostly because his horrendous snoring has now stopped.

I have fallen back in love with the man I married and I could never have imagined a few years ago that that would ever happen. I can't take all the credit; David did a lot of the work too.

I hope you have been encouraged by reading this true account of how we have turned our lives around. I wanted other couples going through the same experience to know that there *is* hope for your relationship. Having a partner on the autistic spectrum is not a death sentence for your marriage.

Endpiece

I thought this would be easy. I had strict instructions from Karen: "Just typeset the book and you can write a little bit at the end, or the beginning or whatever." Well I chose to write a bit at the end. I thought I'd poured out what I could spare from my Aspie-cold-heart out in the previous book; I'd shed a few tears writing my contributions for that, but I had a framework of personal objectivity and a defined viewpoint of almost dispassion and science in that one. I thought that events in this book had been put to one side, forgiven. And they have, but I am still blubbing reading them even knowing there is a sort of happy ending.

I didn't realise at the time what I had done. In my personal copy here on the screen are the apologies and some explanations, but they are for Karen alone. That's the Aspie again – why speak face to face when you can send a text?

Don't take this commentary as negative. Reading through Karen's words expressing the feelings of the time I can see a cycle of ups and downs in our lives. And it's not just one cycle, there are many of them overlapping, interlocking and very, very occasionally all "down" at the same time. Employment and money are tight at the moment: those cycles are down, but love and a mutual understanding are up and seem to be staying that way – those will sustain.

David, May 2017

ACKNOWLEDGEMENTS

Design & Typesetting

David & Karen Rowlands for ARC Publishing. Fonts under license.

FURTHER READING

Attwood, T.; "The Complete Guide to Asperger's Syndrome (Autism Spectrum Disorder): Revised Edition"; Jessica Kingsley Publishers; Paperback edition (15 May 2008); ISBN: 978-1843106692

McCleary, L.; "Feed Your Brain, Lose Your Belly: Experience Dynamic Weight Loss with the Brain-Belly Connection"; Greenleaf Book Group LLC; Hardback 2nd edition (1 April 2011); ISBN: 978-1608321018

Peterson, J.; "Eat Bacon, Don't Jog"; Workman; Paperback 1st edition (21 Nov. 2014); ISBN: 978-0761180548

Rowlands, K.; "Asperger Marriage and Relationships: Insights from the Front Line"; ARC Publishing (Karen Rowlands); Paperback 1st edition (19 April 2016); ISBN: 978-0993561313

All of the above are available for the Kindle e-Book reader through your local Amazon online store

Apps & Online

"Asperger Marriage Instant Help" – Search in the relevant app stores for IoS (Apple) and Android (Samsung etcetera).

Website: http://www.asperger-marriage.com

E-Mail: karen@asperger-marriage.com

44373160R00150

Printed in Poland
by Amazon Fulfillment
Poland Sp. z o.o., Wrocław